MIKE AND MIKE'S
RULES
for Sports and Life

MIKE AND MIKE
ESPN RADIO

MIKE GREENBERG
AND
MIKE GOLIC

WITH ANDREW CHAIKIVSKY

MIKE AND MIKE'S
RULES
for Sports and Life

BALLANTINE BOOKS · NEW YORK

ESPN
BOOKS

Published in the United States by ESPN Books, an imprint of ESPN, Inc., New York, and
Ballantine Books, an imprint of the Random House Publishing Group, a division of
Random House, Inc., New York.

BALLANTINE and colophon are registered trademarks of Random House, Inc.
The ESPN Books name and logo are registered trademarks of ESPN, Inc.

Permission credits can be found on page 243.

ISBN 978-0-345-51622-0

Printed in the United States of America on acid-free paper

www.ballantinebooks.com
www.espnbooks.com

9 8 7 6 5 4 3 2

Design by BTDNYC

This book is for

STACY, NIKKI, AND STEPHEN

and

CHRIS, MIKE, JR., JAKE, AND SYDNEY

because everything we do is for them.

and

FOR ALL OF YOU WHO HAVE STARTED YOUR DAY WITH US,

THROUGH ALL THE SEASONS AND ALL THE SPORTS.

It has been our privilege.

THE CAST

Mike Greenberg	. . .	Greeny
Mike Golic	. . .	Golic
Liam Chapman	. . .	Liam
Curt Kaplan	. . .	Joaquin
Rob Guerrera	. . .	Stats
Scott Shapiro	. . .	The Gnome
Bob Picozzi	. . .	Anchor
Shirley Chapman	. . .	Liam's Mum
Robert Stanbury Olney III	. . .	Buster
Sox	. . .	The Cow
Mark Schlereth	. . .	Stink
Chris Golic	. . .	Golic's wife
Stacy Steponate Greenberg	. . .	Greeny's wife
Arnold Greenberg	. . .	Greeny's dad

THE CHORUS

Matthew Barnaby, Brian Billick, Cris Carter, Bob Costas, Mike Ditka, Peter Gammons, Ron Jaworski, Mel Kiper, Jr., Tim Kurkjian, Erik Kuselias, Tim Legler, Mike Schmidt, Dick Vitale, Trey Wingo

THE CONTENTS

FIRST HOUR

In which the Mikes get their act together . . . The fans shout for more . . . Greeny reveals his great

commandment . . . Home runs don't count . . . Bud Selig changes his mind . . . Greeny throws out

the challenge flag . . . The Mikes play tag . . . A pitcher gets spooked . . . Letters arrive in the

mailbox . . . Terry Francona gets undressed . . . and Greeny plans Lou Piniella's wardrobe.

> **PLUS: Remote (and Out of) Control; Greeny's "12 for '12"; and more rules.**

SECOND HOUR

In which Golic makes a rookie mistake . . . The Mikes find a pot of gold . . . Stats schools K-Rod . . .

Michael Phelps goes Hollywood . . . The Mikes sleep through *Jaws* . . . A golfer makes a shocking

confession . . . Greeny does something about the weather . . . Golic goes on a bounty hunt . . .

Cris Carter's got milk . . . LeBron James storms off . . . The Mikes shake hands, almost . . .

Dick Vitale gives a pep talk . . . and Greeny goes shopping.

> **PLUS: The Mike and Mike Pentathlon; Just Pick a Number; and even more rules.**

THIRD HOUR

In which Golic takes to the stands, dude . . . The Gnome disagrees . . . Greeny's father instructs the

Mikes . . . A perfect moment is *ixnayed* . . . Golic meets Gravlax . . . A fan calls out Reggie White . . .

The accusations fly . . . Golic talks steroids . . . Bob Costas offers some sage advice . . . and

the Mikes crush a quarterback, sort of.

> **PLUS: Sheets of Integrity; Never Forget Where You Came From; and, yes, a few rules for**
>
> **milking a cow.**

FOREWORD by George Will

AMERICANS must be the most argumentative people on the planet. Others compete for that title—the Serbs and Bosnians, the Sunnis and Shia, the Catholics and Protestants of Northern Ireland. All of these folks, however, have the unfortunate habit of trying to strengthen their arguments with bombs and bullets, which should be against the rules.

In America, where argument is the national pastime, resorting to gunfire is a disqualification. The insistence on disarmament does not matter so much when Americans are arguing only about politics, religion, and other matters of marginal importance. But mutually assured destruction must be avoided when the subject of debate is the stuff that involves Americans' deepest convictions and most molten passions. I refer, of course, to sports.

Which brings us to the Abraham Lincoln and Stephen Douglas of sports debating—the two Mikes, Greenberg and Golic. They both probably want to be understood as the Lincoln in this equivalency. But Greenberg is not tall (neither was Douglas) and Golic is not thin (neither was Douglas).

What they agree about, I am sure, is that they have the best job in America. They are actually paid to do what the rest of us do for the fun of it—talk about sports. The rest of us, just like Mike and Mike, lay down the law, pound the table, and hurl statistics like harmless hand grenades. Like the Mikes, we are often in error but never in doubt. Unlike them, we have to have other jobs. Life really is unfair.

Actually, the Mikes are not quite mere observers of, and commentators on, the sports scene. They have become, in a sense, umpires or referees. There is so much naked nonsense on sports talk radio, and in the blogosphere, so much dumb meanness, that the temptation is to turn it all off and read Proust. (I can't do that now. Golic has borrowed my *Remembrance of Things Past* and refuses to return it.) But the Mikes manage to be an island—perhaps two islands—of informed civility in a sea of bloviation.

This matters, a lot. Every sector of American society should be held to reasonable standards of discourse. It is a sobering fact that the Mikes set standards of informativeness and politeness to which political argument rarely rises.

Mark Twain said that the first thing you should do every morning is swallow a live frog, so you will know that the worst part of your day is over. More than a century later, the first thing you should do every morning is tune in the Mikes: It might be the last moment in the day when you are able to be in the company of two smart and funny people.

Of course, you can only do that on weekdays. What, then, of the barren stretch known as the weekend? Presumably, that is what this book is for, to carry you over until you can exclaim, "TGIM!"—Thank God it's Monday. I am going to read and reread it until Golic returns my Proust.

PREFACE by Kenny Chesney

WHEN you live on the road, you can count on this: every day, you're somewhere else, but it almost always looks the same. The parking lots. The locker rooms. The backstage hallways. When you live like that, you look for things you can count on no matter where you are to make you feel alive, to get your day started with a jolt of energy, passion, heart.

That's why I started listening to—and watching—*Mike and Mike* out on the road. Not because there isn't enough ESPN in our world, but more because I think most guys are a bit like the both of them. Mike Golic is the professional athlete who knows how the game is played. Mike Greenberg is the journalist who's not afraid to be a fan who lives and dies for the game even though he'll never get to suit up and get out there. Both are men who exist for the competition, the love of sports and—honestly—making fun of each other.

In a world where the band and I live to play—often in the same NFL stadiums where these teams thrill us every fall, Mike and Mike get the intensity that is also the rock 'n' roll life, whether you're onstage or in the stands. Golic knows and talks about the way it feels to be right there when the plays go down, what those pressures are, how great it is when everything comes together, the importance of the camaraderie in the locker room. Greenberg speaks the truth of how powerful watching sports can be, how much it means to the fan and why it matters.

'Cause that's the thing: being a fan matters. I still love Aerosmith and Bruce Springsteen, just like I love the passion of Dick Vitale, the history of Fenway Park, Wrigley Field, and the old Yankee Stadium, the tradition of the Tennessee Volunteers and the determination of Sean Payton and just about every team that gets out there and plays hard. It takes a lot of sacrifice and commitment to play sports at the level of the people Mike and Mike are talking about, but there's also a lot of humanity that goes into it, too.

If there's one thing Golic and Greenberg get, it's that these players are the very best of the best, and what they do isn't just something to talk about, but to celebrate. They fight, they cheer, they debate, but mostly, they love sports the same way we all do.

It's the one thing we can count on. And to see people bringing as much heart and passion to what they do as I'd like to think we do, well, that's all you can ask first thing in the morning after a long night somewhere else, bringing people's summer and memories alive.

For me, and for a lotta the people out here on the road with me, Mike and Mike are a couple of buddies who may not agree, but who know how to argue like the best of friends. They're also the kind of people who know all the stats, the players, the history, and the competitive nature of sports. Plus, they have a crazy sense of humor.

As long as there's mornings, I hope Mike and Mike will be on the air. It's a reason to get going when all you wanna do is turn over and sleep off the night before.

RULE 1.28:

Baseball Managers Should Dress Like Normal People.

 GREENY: What a great game our national pastime is, a sport of skill, athleticism, strategy, explosive action, and great suspense. Every baseball game starts exactly the same, perfect and pristine in those expectant moments before the first pitch, and then it's . . . *Play ball!* . . . A swing and a miss . . . the diving catch . . . the hard slide, a cloud of dust, and a stolen base . . .

GOLIC: The peanuts, the Cracker Jack, a beer and a hot dog.

GREENY: Wait, wait, wait. . . . What are you doing?

GOLIC: I'm talking about baseball, helping you out.

GREENY: No you're not. You're not helping. You're *interrupting.* How long have we been doing the show together?

GOLIC: About four years?

GREENY: *Ten* years, and during those ten years you've been constantly interrupting me, day in and day out. Now we're writing a book about our rules for sports, and what do you do? On the *very first page*? I can't believe this is happening. What is wrong with you?

GOLIC: Calm down . . . Okay, I'm sorry. Go ahead.

GREENY: Thank you.

What a great game our national pastime is, a sport of athleticism and strategy, explosive action and great suspense. Every baseball game starts exactly the

GOLIC: Everyone's read that part already, Greeny.

GREENY: There you go again. . . . Look, I've spent a lot of time writing this, and I think they'll like it. It's good, and I should start it from the beginning.

GOLIC: So do that. Just tell everyone about the 2002 All-Star Game and how you came up with the dumbest rule in sports.

RULE 1.05

Radio? Fun. Cartoons? Even more fun.

We'll be kicking off each hour with a cartoon from the folks at Animax, who won a 2006 Broadband Emmy for *Off Mikes,* the animated series that took snippets from our show and turned them into episodes on ESPN.com. They did all the work. We'll take all the credit.

GREENY: It's a great rule, Mike.

GOLIC: Here's how it happened: It was the day after the 2002 All-Star Game, the one that was called after 11 innings because both teams ran out of players—no winner, no loser, nothing. Everyone was shaking their heads that morning and asking, What the heck?

But what else could they do? The fans were frustrated—the crowd at the game began chanting "Let them play" just like the fans did in the Houston Astrodome in the second *Bad News Bears* movie. The way it ended sure was bad news, but what other options were there?

GREENY: I'm disappointed to hear you say that, because I completely agree with you. With every fiber of my being and with every ounce in my soul, I want to tell you that you're wrong. But in this instance I can't. There was simply no other solution.

It's very easy to criticize someone by saying that they should have done something different, but it's much, *much* harder to come up with exactly what that something should be. The managers of the All-Star Game believe that their goal is to get every player into the game, and they assume that they have nine innings to do it. So if the game goes longer, there will come a time when they simply won't have anyone left. What else can you do? If the NBA All-Star Game goes into overtime, the players might get tired, but who cares; it's not a crisis. Not so in baseball. No All-Star manager wants to inform a team that's in the middle of a division race that its pitching ace is going to miss his next three starts because he's got a stiff arm on account of the All-Star Game running longer than usual.

GOLIC: The biggest shame was that it had all the makings of a great night, so to have it end in a tie is a huge disappointment. You go to a baseball game expecting it will end with some kind of conclusion, and it doesn't.

GREENY: But it did have a conclusion: It concluded in a tie. The real shame is that they've been calling it the All-Star Game since the very first one in 1933. You have to define it for what it really is. It is not a baseball game—it's an exhibition of baseball that's played in a format similar to what we're accustomed to seeing the rest of the year. When I first brought this up with you—a whole *year* before the 2002 debacle, no less—I was laughed at. I was slaughtered for it. Let's go to the tape:

> **GREENY:** Who cares if the American League or the National League wins the All-Star Game? If they want to keep calling it a game, put some juice in it. Make it count for something, like home field advantage in the World Series.
>
> **GOLIC:** You're an idiot. That's so stupid, I'm going to pretend you didn't say it. It's never going to happen, and you've just wasted 30 seconds of my life.
>
> **MIKE AND MIKE IN THE MORNING,**
> **July 2001**

GREENY: So imagine everyone's surprise—except mine—when Major League Baseball announced that, starting in 2003, the All-Star Game would determine home field advantage in the World Series. I was right! And you know what the best part of it is? That you were wrong.

RULE 1.08(a)

The Greeny Rule

The team representing the winning league of the All-Star Game will be awarded a one-game home field advantage in the World Series.

RULE 1.08(b)

Earn it.

GOLIC: You've played 162 games during the regular season, you have the best record in the majors, but you don't get home field advantage in the World Series because some add-on to the All-Star roster from the other league singled home the winning run in a ceremonial game back in July. Are you *kidding* me?

The winner of the All-Star Game earns bragging rights. And that's more than enough.

GOLIC: Every sport has rules that are known for the people who were responsible for the rule change. Like the Sean Avery Rule in hockey. In football, you've got the Deacon Jones Rule outlawing head slaps. Now baseball has the Greeny Rule. But that doesn't mean I have to agree with it. I don't. I still think it's the dumbest thing I've ever heard. It's like the Mendoza Line— nothing to be proud of.

SHORTSTOP MARIANERS
MARIO MENDOZA
TOPPS

GREENY: Major League Baseball heeded my advice, so the new format for the All-Star Game will forever be known as the Greeny Rule—kind of like the Pythagorean theorem in geometry, but different. All the credit goes to me because I say it does.

Do you realize how hard it is to get baseball to change anything? Granted, no major professional sport does history better. It's baseball's place in our society. It's a part of our culture. Show me a clip of Willie Mays or Hank Aaron or Joe DiMaggio, and it's impossible not to feel the swell in your chest. But baseball does not do the present well. Take video review. All the other major sports have been using instant replay for years and with great success (for the most part). But baseball? Stuck in the past.

Ban the Red Flag.

GREENY: The NFL's challenge system? The league should get rid of it. Right now.

If a blatantly bad call is made on the field, it shouldn't be up to a head coach to determine whether or not it will be corrected. Coaches should coach, and officials should officiate.

Even worse, the NFL insists that, unless it's the last two minutes of the half or the game, the head coach has to have a timeout in order to request a review. (The NFL's rule is that if a coach challenges a call and he's wrong, he loses a timeout. No timeouts left, no challenges allowed.) Nothing brought the idiocy of this system to light better than the conclusion of a game a couple of years ago between the Falcons and the Eagles. After scoring a touchdown late in the fourth quarter to pull them to within six points of the Eagles at 20–14, the Falcons held the Eagles to a three-and-out with about 2:30 left on the clock. The Eagles punt. Adam Jennings, the return man, starts up for the ball and then stops; he sees that he won't be able to get to it. The ball bounces in front of him, bounces in the air, and then an Eagles player grabs it. The refs rule that Jennings touched the ball, making the play a muffed punt and giving Philadelphia possession. On the very first replay they show on TV, everyone can clearly see that Jennings never touched the ball. So you're waiting for Mike Smith, the Falcons' head coach, to throw the red flag. Trust me, he wanted to. But he couldn't. He was out of timeouts—he had used all three to stop the clock during the Eagles' three-and-out possession.

It was an easily reversible call, an obvious mistake made by the officials on the field, and everyone knew it.

Instead of the Falcons driving to try for a game-winning touchdown, the Eagles retained the ball, and Brian Westbrook broke off on a 39-yard TD run, and suddenly the Eagles were up by 13, and the game was over.

It shouldn't be so complicated. Reverse any bad call, period. Thank you very much.

RULE 1.10(a)

The "human element" in officiating sucks.

RULE 1.10(b)

The Mike and Mike Rule

All bad calls that can be corrected, should be.

GOLIC: Baseball purists can talk all they want about the charm of the human element of the game, but what's the advantage in having a team lose because of a blown call? They already have cameras in every ballpark.

GREENY: A couple of years ago, we brought Bud Selig on the show, and we went on and on about this with him. Clearly, he was against the use of video replay. "But there are certainly a lot of voices on the other side of it," he said. He was referring to the two of us, obviously. Several weeks later, he reversed course and announced that baseball would start using video review on a limited basis for home run calls only. What changed his mind? We did, of course, and the Mike and Mike Rule was born.

GOLIC: Well, what also helped was the fact that within a single week there were three horrific calls on home runs that were just blatantly wrong. On a Sunday night, Carlos Delgado hit a shot that bounced off the left field foul pole, but the umpires incorrectly ruled it a foul ball. The next day, Geovany Soto of the Cubs hit a home run, but the umps couldn't see if the ball had actually cleared the wall or not. It did, but the ruling on the field was that it had not. Two days after that, they took a home run away from A-Rod. So there it was—three blown calls in four days. But we'd been going off on it for a while, too.

GREENY: For years we've been getting on baseball's case about video replay. In fairness to us, they should put up signage in every major league ballpark that reads, "The Mike and Mike Replay." We should take it a step further and have them put my face in fair territory and your face in foul and start

referring to a ball as either "a greeny" or "a golic." From now on, they'll say, "Dustin Pedroia golicked off seven pitches before he greenied one down the left field line for a triple."

Clearly I should be fair, because I'm known for being fair. And as anyone who's ever been around you knows, you can be somewhat foul, especially during the warmer summer months.

GOLIC: You're right. I can be foul.

GREENY: But the Mike and Mike Rule, which we've been screaming about for years, isn't just for home runs. There's a lot you can easily catch on tape, and instant replay should be used to correct the *obvious* missed call. Overturning it would take about five seconds. *Five seconds!* If they look at the play from several different angles and they're still not sure—if, to borrow the term from the NFL, they can't find "indisputable visual evidence"—then the call on the field is close enough. It's not the end of the world. Either it's a home run or it's not. He's safe or he's out. He caught the ball, or he trapped it. Make the right call and let's get on with life.

Look at how well it works in the NFL. Everyone's going to point to the one call in the NFL where it didn't work—like Ed Hochuli's infamous call in the Denver game in '08—but how many bad calls have been overturned by instant replay on whether or not a player has possession of the ball? And you could have the same thing in baseball.

GOLIC: In the Hochuli play, instant replay didn't work because they weren't allowed to use it. He'd blown the whistle.

GREENY: That's what I mean. There was one small instance that instant replay couldn't correct the call, but that's compared to the hundreds of calls that instant replay *is* able to correct.

GOLIC: Look, I'm as much a proponent of instant replay as you are. Do I want them to dive in with both feet and replay everything? Absolutely not. But what I think baseball could do is try replay out in the spring training games for more than just home run calls. Doesn't mean you have to put it in place once the regular season starts, but I think that's where you need to start trying. Try it. It can't hurt.

GREENY: Those are two good, new rules. But our work is not done, because there are other rules in baseball that I wouldn't necessarily want changed, I simply want them clarified. I want them to make sense. Take the rule on tags, for example.

GOLIC: **What's your problem? Everyone knows what a tag is.**

GREENY: Let's look at what the official rulebook of Major League Baseball has to say about it. ───────────────────►

> A tag is the action of a fielder in touching a base with his body while holding the ball securely and firmly in his hand or glove; or touching the runner with the ball, or with his hand or glove holding the ball, while holding the ball securely and firmly in his hand or glove.
>
> **Official Baseball Rules,**
> **Rule 2.00**
> **Definition of terms**

GOLIC: **Man, that's a lot of words.**

GREENY: For you it is, so I'll translate: If you hold the ball securely and touch the runner with it or touch the base, he's out.

GOLIC: **See, that isn't always true. Take a collision at the plate, like Pete Rose blowing up Ray Fosse in the All-Star Game. If that is indeed the rule, then Pete Rose and every other runner should be out if the catcher has the ball—"firmly and securely," like the rulebook says—even if he gets blown up as he makes the tag and loses the ball. If the umpire calls the runner safe, then according to the exact words in the rulebook, it's the wrong call.**

GREENY: I think in that case, an argument can be made that the runner jarred the ball loose.

GOLIC: It doesn't say that in the rules.

GREENY: I understand that, but if the runner jars the ball loose, did the catcher really have the ball securely when the tag was being made? If I am tagging you, and I've got the ball securely and I touch you with the ball, and in my touching you, you knock it right out of my mitt, then I didn't really have it when I touched you, did I?

GOLIC: If you're the catcher and I'm coming around to score, you really think you're holding on to the ball? Or are you curling up in a fetal position before I round third?

GREENY: That's not the point.

GOLIC: Okay, but let's say—just for the sake of argument—that there's a play at the plate, you have the ball in your mitt, you get completely run over but you somehow manage to hold on to the ball "firmly and securely." You hit the ground, and *then* the ball comes loose and pops out. What's the call? The runner is safe. Always.

Don't get me wrong—that's the correct call. But it seems that if you go by the exact words of the official rulebook, you're not so sure.

GREENY: Rules should be easy to understand and simple to follow, and one obvious advantage of the Mike and Mike Rule is its clarity. Nine simple words. What's more, rules should be written down. No doubt baseball has more unwritten rules than any other sport, but they only serve to complicate things, which is the exact opposite of what good rules are meant to do. Which unwritten rules am I supposed to follow? Which ones is the other guy following? Is he getting pissed off at me because I broke an unwritten rule that he's keeping and I'm not? Which rule? It's maddening.

GOLIC: Most unwritten rules are plain stupid. I've heard that batters aren't supposed to celebrate after hitting a home run—they should just put their head down and circle the bases. Get real! I'm not saying you should taunt the pitcher or start jumping up and down when your team's down by 10 runs, but what's wrong with showing some emotion?

RULE 1.15

The unwritten rules of baseball are not written down for a reason.

GREENY: Another unwritten rule is that you shouldn't try to bunt your way on during a no-hitter. That's what Ben Davis of the Padres found out after he bunted his way to first base in the eighth inning of Curt Schilling's bid for a perfect game in 2001. Schilling, who was pitching for the Diamondbacks then, was livid, and so was his manager, Bob Brenly. But the Padres were only down 2–0 at that point, and if Davis gets on base, the tying run is at the plate. You're trying to win the game! And for some reason that's not right?

GOLIC: So if I'm leading off a game—it's a no-hitter at that point, and a perfect game, too—I can't try to bunt my way on?

GREENY: Gee, I don't know. Let's look it up. Oh wait—that's an unwritten rule. Never mind.

WHEN WE COME BACK ON PAGE 18, THE ONE THING ABOUT BASEBALL *EVERYONE* SHOULD BE AFRAID TO TALK ABOUT.

REMOTE (AND OUT OF) CONTROL
Here's what happens when you take the show on the road.

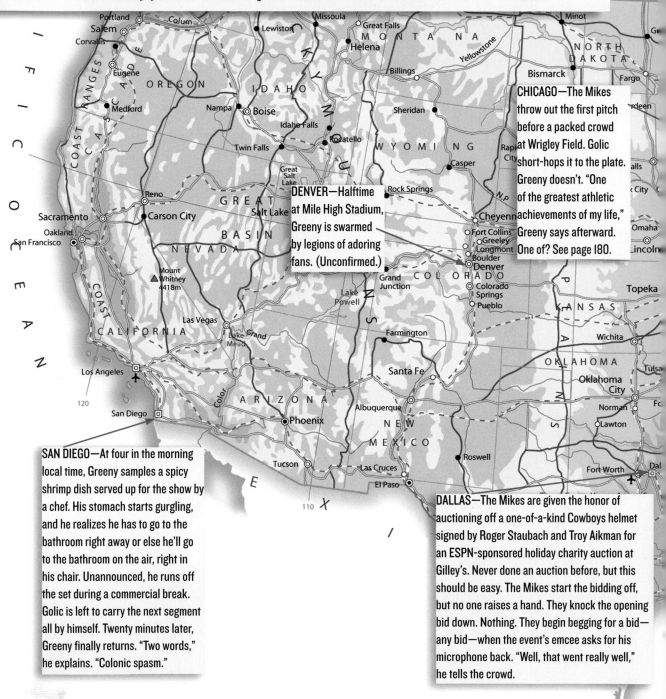

CHICAGO—The Mikes throw out the first pitch before a packed crowd at Wrigley Field. Golic short-hops it to the plate. Greeny doesn't. "One of the greatest athletic achievements of my life," Greeny says afterward. One of? See page 180.

DENVER—Halftime at Mile High Stadium, Greeny is swarmed by legions of adoring fans. (Unconfirmed.)

SAN DIEGO—At four in the morning local time, Greeny samples a spicy shrimp dish served up for the show by a chef. His stomach starts gurgling, and he realizes he has to go to the bathroom right away or else he'll go to the bathroom on the air, right in his chair. Unannounced, he runs off the set during a commercial break. Golic is left to carry the next segment all by himself. Twenty minutes later, Greeny finally returns. "Two words," he explains. "Colonic spasm."

DALLAS—The Mikes are given the honor of auctioning off a one-of-a-kind Cowboys helmet signed by Roger Staubach and Troy Aikman for an ESPN-sponsored holiday charity auction at Gilley's. Never done an auction before, but this should be easy. The Mikes start the bidding off, but no one raises a hand. They knock the opening bid down. Nothing. They begin begging for a bid—any bid—when the event's emcee asks for his microphone back. "Well, that went really well," he tells the crowd.

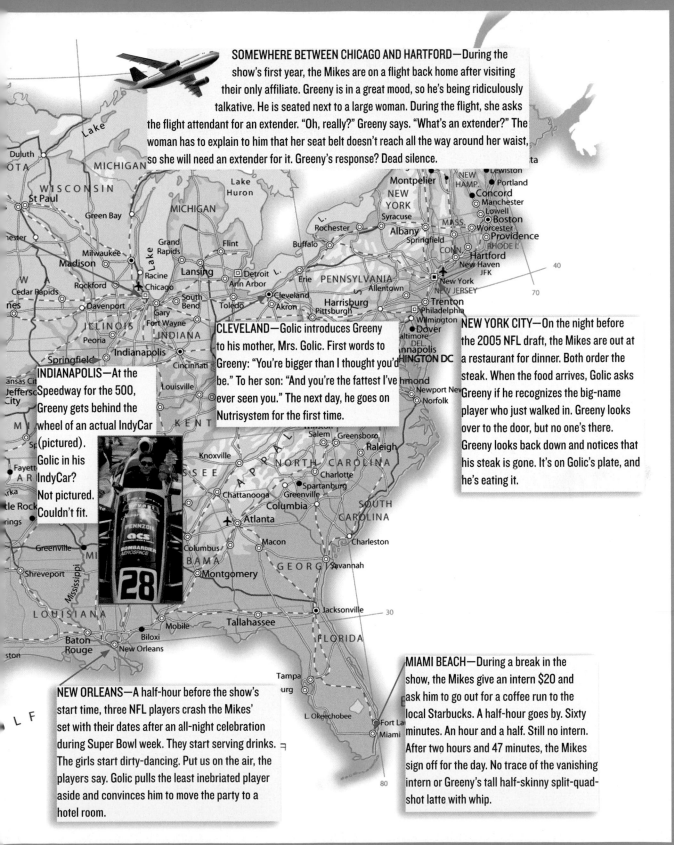

SOMEWHERE BETWEEN CHICAGO AND HARTFORD—During the show's first year, the Mikes are on a flight back home after visiting their only affiliate. Greeny is in a great mood, so he's being ridiculously talkative. He is seated next to a large woman. During the flight, she asks the flight attendant for an extender. "Oh, really?" Greeny says. "What's an extender?" The woman has to explain to him that her seat belt doesn't reach all the way around her waist, so she will need an extender for it. Greeny's response? Dead silence.

CLEVELAND—Golic introduces Greeny to his mother, Mrs. Golic. First words to Greeny: "You're bigger than I thought you'd be." To her son: "And you're the fattest I've ever seen you." The next day, he goes on Nutrisystem for the first time.

NEW YORK CITY—On the night before the 2005 NFL draft, the Mikes are out at a restaurant for dinner. Both order the steak. When the food arrives, Golic asks Greeny if he recognizes the big-name player who just walked in. Greeny looks over to the door, but no one's there. Greeny looks back down and notices that his steak is gone. It's on Golic's plate, and he's eating it.

INDIANAPOLIS—At the Speedway for the 500, Greeny gets behind the wheel of an actual IndyCar (pictured). Golic in his IndyCar? Not pictured. Couldn't fit.

NEW ORLEANS—A half-hour before the show's start time, three NFL players crash the Mikes' set with their dates after an all-night celebration during Super Bowl week. They start serving drinks. The girls start dirty-dancing. Put us on the air, the players say. Golic pulls the least inebriated player aside and convinces him to move the party to a hotel room.

MIAMI BEACH—During a break in the show, the Mikes give an intern $20 and ask him to go out for a coffee run to the local Starbucks. A half-hour goes by. Sixty minutes. An hour and a half. Still no intern. After two hours and 47 minutes, the Mikes sign off for the day. No trace of the vanishing intern or Greeny's tall half-skinny split-quad-shot latte with whip.

But there is one unwritten rule that I think everyone can agree on, even the both of us. It's this: If your pitcher has a no-hitter going, don't mention it to him. Better yet, don't even talk to him. Wouldn't you agree?

GOLIC: No. When I was playing in the NFL, I wouldn't bug a kicker who was about to kick a field goal—I'd just leave him alone. Let him do his thing. But if someone else from the team walked over and started talking to him, I wouldn't start freaking out. It's no different with baseball and pitchers.

GREENY: It is different, and you're clearly a lunatic. What you're telling me is that it's okay to spit in the face of the baseball gods.

RULE 1.18

Don't neglect the golf gods, either.

Triputtus
Sirena Submergus   THE GODS of GOLF   Santrapius
Treehooksus

GREENY: Several holes into a round, you notice that you're playing well. Really well. In fact, you're playing great. So you do the math: If you can hold par on half of the remaining holes and make birdies on the rest, you're going to shoot the best round of your life. Even if you hit par from here on in, you'll smoke everyone in your foursome. Awesome. You start thinking about Q-School again, sending out for an application, and definitely erasing those files from your hard drive at work before you quit your job and play the Tour full-time.

And then it happens. You slice your very next shot into the trees. Three strokes later, you're in the drink. You four-putt the green. Two more holes and you realize that this has now turned into your worst round. Ever.

What gives? Where did your game go?

It's the golf gods. Tempt them by figuring out your score ahead of time or even by *thinking* you're playing well, and they'll make you pay. Every time.

GOLIC: That's not what I'm saying at all, because there's no such thing.

GREENY: Mike, it's one of the oldest, most respected traditions in baseball. You simply cannot mention a no-hitter. Now, I've heard it suggested that even announcers shouldn't bring it up during the broadcast, but I totally disagree. As an announcer, it's your job to tell the story of the game to people who may otherwise not know it (with one exception). Outside of that, don't mention it. Don't confront the pitcher with it—in any way. In June 2009, Cliff Lee of the Indians was pitching a no-hitter at home through seven innings against the Cardinals. As he was taking the mound for the top of the eighth, a trivia question flashed on the scoreboard: Who was the last Indians pitcher to throw a perfect game? On the next pitch—the *very* next pitch—Yadier Molina hit a solid double off the right field wall. So let me ask you: Wasn't the scoreboard operator wrong to put that question up?

RULE 1.19

Stop jinxing my team.

GREENY: It's March Madness, second round, and the team you've picked to go on to the Sweet 16 is at the line with under a second remaining on the clock. They're down by one. It's make-or-break time. Does everyone need to know that your guy hasn't missed a free throw in his last 14 attempts? The answer is a clear and resounding no, because as soon as the announcer mentions it, you're screwed.

Trust me.

And one more thing: If you're ever announcing a Jets game and find yourself tempted to let everybody know that our kicker hasn't missed a field goal since the Roosevelt administration, my advice is: Don't. Thank you.

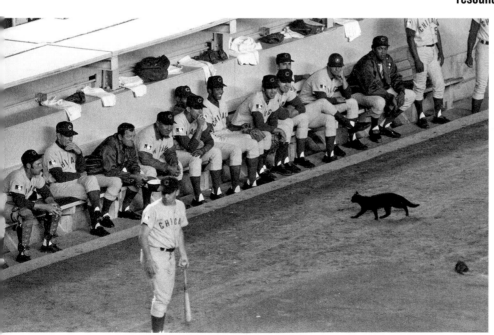

ON THE MIKES

By Mike Schmidt, THREE-TIME NL MVP AND HALL OF FAME
THIRD BASEMAN

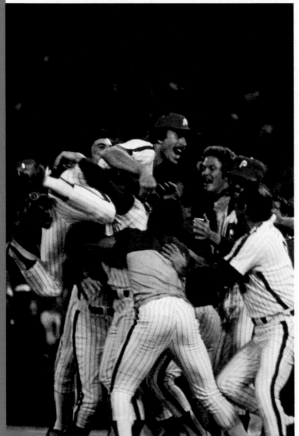

Right after the final out of the 1980 World Series, I started jumping up and down and hugging the first teammates I saw. Soon we were all piling on top of each another. The fans can see that, but they don't realize what the players are feeling deep down: pure love for one another. I know it sounds strange, but that's what I felt. It's what every guy feels. For seven long months, you've been living together, traveling together, hanging out in hotel rooms together, playing cards together, cheering each other on, suffering together. You've forged a very special brotherhood with these men, and when it culminates in the ultimate victory, when you've reached the top of the mountain together, you've surely got some serious love for one another. It's not something you ever talk about, but all these men are hugging you and are whispering in your ear about how much they love you.

—MIKE AND MIKE IN THE MORNING,
October 28, 2008

RULE 1.20: Winning is all about love.

GOLIC: No, he wasn't. It had nothing to do with the scoreboard operator. If you're looking for the person who's responsible for breaking up the no-hitter, start with the guy who had the bat in his hands.

GREENY: It's absolutely the scoreboard operator's fault. If it's in your own stadium and you've got a no-hitter going, you don't ask a no-hitter trivia question. It's a rule. Let me be clear: I am not saying that the scoreboard operator should have been fired. I'm saying that he should have been arrested.

You know, our inbox has been getting lots of messages. People seem to have strong opinions about this.

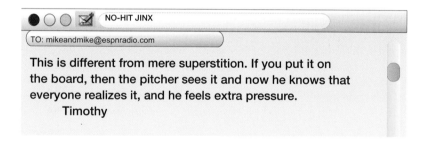

NO-HIT JINX

TO: mikeandmike@espnradio.com

This is different from mere superstition. If you put it on the board, then the pitcher sees it and now he knows that everyone realizes it, and he feels extra pressure.
Timothy

GOLIC: You're right, Tim. Cliff Lee saw the trivia question and thought, "Oh my God! Now everyone knows!" In fact, nobody in the entire stadium realized it before then, and they were all completely stunned. Lee had no choice but to throw an 82-mile-an-hour fastball that Molina smacked for a double.

GREENY: Timothy may not be the best advocate for my side.

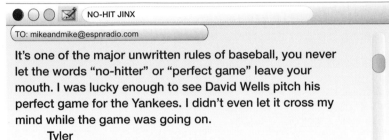

○ ○ ○ ✉ NO-HIT JINX

TO: mikeandmike@espnradio.com

It's one of the major unwritten rules of baseball, you never let the words "no-hitter" or "perfect game" leave your mouth. I was lucky enough to see David Wells pitch his perfect game for the Yankees. I didn't even let it cross my mind while the game was going on.
Tyler
Wilkes-Barre, Pennsylvania

GOLIC: I hope David Wells sent you a big fruit basket, Tyler, because without you, he would've never thrown a perfect game.

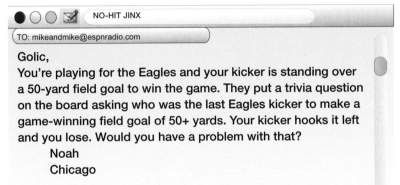

○ ○ ○ ✉ NO-HIT JINX

TO: mikeandmike@espnradio.com

Golic,
You're playing for the Eagles and your kicker is standing over a 50-yard field goal to win the game. They put a trivia question on the board asking who was the last Eagles kicker to make a game-winning field goal of 50+ yards. Your kicker hooks it left and you lose. Would you have a problem with that?
Noah
Chicago

GOLIC: It's not the scoreboard's fault, nor the guy who put it on the scoreboard. It's not what the announcer said or didn't say, or whether you were sitting a certain way, standing on one leg, holding a beer in your left hand, whatever. It has nothing to do with the kick. Jeez! It's like I'm slamming my head against a wall.

GREENY: You're wrong, though, and I'll tell you why. Obviously, Cliff Lee knew he was throwing a no-hitter. But anything that takes you out of the mind-set of concentrating on your next pitch can affect your performance. If Cliff Lee saw the trivia question, I really do believe that it could have gone through his mind that they probably shouldn't have put it up there. There's a whole tradition in baseball that strongly believes that. And all of a sudden, instead of making sure that your slider is breaking two feet off the plate, you've got a million other things going through your mind.

GOLIC: I don't care if Lee walked off the mound, climbed up to the stadium announcer's booth, got on the mike, and said, "Hey, I know—it's Len Barker, and he did it on May 15, 1981," and then threw his next pitch. He's not a seven-year-old who's going to mentally disintegrate because he sees something on the scoreboard. And if he did get rattled by that question, then that tells me a hell of a lot about Cliff Lee.

GREENY: What about this? No one will dispute the fact that Tiger Woods is one of the greatest golfers the game has ever seen, if not the best. He wears red on Sundays. For whatever reason, he's decided that it makes him feel comfortable. It helps him. Is that a superstition? You don't think there's any correlation between him wearing red and playing better?

GOLIC: It's called a routine. If you do something a bunch of times and you have success with it, why change it? It's one less thing to worry about.

GREENY: If you're trying to tell me that you don't believe in any of this stuff— the gods of baseball, the golf gods, kismet, fate—then why is it that every time you're driving somewhere and you're making great time, if you dare mention it, you're sure to find yourself backed up in the worst traffic jam ever.

GOLIC: You're nuts.

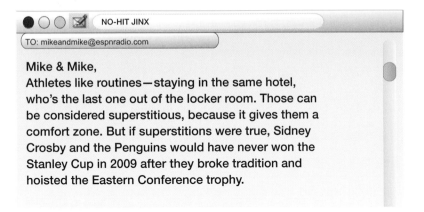

NO-HIT JINX

TO: mikeandmike@espnradio.com

Mike & Mike,
Athletes like routines—staying in the same hotel,
who's the last one out of the locker room. Those can
be considered superstitious, because it gives them a
comfort zone. But if superstitions were true, Sidney
Crosby and the Penguins would have never won the
Stanley Cup in 2009 after they broke tradition and
hoisted the Eastern Conference trophy.

GREENY: When you were playing at Notre Dame—I realize that they didn't have the "Play Like A Champion" sign up then, that the sign and the tradition of touching it as you're heading out onto the field was brought back later by Lou Holtz—would you have touched the sign?

GOLIC: You know, I probably would have, but not because of superstition. Let's say I forgot to touch it before a game; there's no way I'm going to head back into the locker room and start taking my pads off because, hey, how in the world am I going to shake off a block after I forgot to touch the sign? Stop it. I would touch the sign because it's a tradition that builds unity among the players on the team, and I'd want everyone to feel that. It could come in handy during a goal line stand late in the fourth quarter.

GREENY: Some traditions are important, but many of them are senseless. For example, in baseball, you have managers wearing uniforms. Why? And why does the league even concern itself with this? Terry Francona, the manager of the Red Sox, got into the habit of wearing a pullover, but a couple of years ago during a game against the Yankees—I repeat, *during* a game, with the Yankees batting and Derek Jeter on second—a league representative came into the dugout, pulled Francona aside, and checked under his pullover to make sure he was wearing a uniform. Needless to say, Francona wasn't happy about it.

GOLIC: I'm with Francona. Do it before or after the game or, at the very least, do it between innings.

GREENY: I can just imagine it. "Terry, what are you wearing under there? Under where? Ha ha!" It must have made all the kids laugh. But I'm taking this a step further: Why do managers wear uniforms anyway? Phil Jackson doesn't have to wear a tank top and shorts on the sidelines. Bill Belichick isn't wearing shoulder pads. But in baseball, there are 70-year-old men walking around in baseball pants, stirrups, even cleats. Why are Joe Torre or Charlie Manuel wearing a uniform? It looks nonsensical. I've never been to a sumo wrestling match, but I'd love to know if they make sumo coaches wear the big diapers.

GOLIC: I don't know if there's another sport where the coaches have to wear the uniform.

GREENY: It's pointless. Right in the middle of a game, the league went and checked on something that makes no sense to begin with.

RULE 1.26

Get rid of the Fourth of July.

GOLIC: I can tell you already that I'm going to veto this one.

GREENY: Just give me a chance to explain it. Okay, it's summer, and the Fourth of July is coming up. You notice that it falls on a Wednesday, smack dab in the middle of the week. What's your reaction?

GOLIC: Confusion.

GREENY: That's always your reaction.

GOLIC: Shut up. It's confusing because unless the Fourth is on a Monday or a Friday, you don't know what days off people are going to be taking. So if it's on Tuesday, are you going to work on the Monday? If it's on a Wednesday, can you take the Monday and Tuesday off, or the Thursday and Friday? And when the Fourth of July falls on a Saturday or Sunday, you don't know if you're going to get the Friday off, or the Monday, or neither.

GREENY: That's my point. We should stop attaching the Fourth of July to a specific day. It just doesn't work.

GOLIC: But it's the Fourth of July.

GREENY: I've looked into this, and in 1776, the Fourth of July—the actual date—fell on a Thursday. Why don't we celebrate our nation's independence every year on the first Thursday in July? Everyone will get Thursday and Friday off, and then it's the weekend.

GOLIC: But then what's the holiday if it's not the Fourth of July?

GREENY: We'll call it what it is: Independence Day. Every year, on the first Thursday in July we'll eat a hot dog, drink a beer, and shoot fireworks, and then get three more days off.

GOLIC: You know, I like it. Much less complicated.

GREENY: I'm saying it right now: The Fourth of July, its time has come and gone. Let's make it the first Thursday in July and get on with our lives.

GOLIC: In the NFL, the fashion police check before every game, usually during warmups, to make sure everything is legit.

GREENY: Check who?

GOLIC: They check the players.

GREENY: The players!

GOLIC: Yes, they check coaches, too, especially these days. They have to make sure that the coach is wearing the right product, like an officially licensed ballcap. It's ridiculous.

GREENY: I hate to say it, but I can understand that. The team or league signs a clothing deal, so there's a financial reason behind it. But with baseball, how many people run out and buy a Tigers uniform because they've seen Jim Leyland wearing one? Put him in a suit and sell that.

RULE 1.27

Steroids aside, McGwire and Sosa never "saved" baseball.

GREENY: I hear this one all the time. McGwire and Sosa came along in the wake of the worst players' strike in the history of major American sports and saved baseball. What? This was three years after Cal Ripken broke Lou Gehrig's record for consecutive games played, which brought an enormous amount of positive attention to the game. But Cal Ripken didn't save baseball—and neither did McGwire or Sosa—because baseball didn't *need* saving. These players just happened to do something after the strike that galvanized everyone's attention. If they hadn't done it, someone or something else would have. The notion that any one player—or two players—can do anything to rescue an institution like baseball is crazy. Had Mark McGwire and Sammy Sosa not hit those home runs in 1998, would Major League Baseball have gone the way of the North American Soccer League? Would the fans have stayed away for good? Would we all have just stopped caring?

GOLIC: I wouldn't want to see managers in the dugout in their Sunday best, not with all the spitting that goes on. They should be casually dressed. Or they could wear a lot of the cool, team-related stuff that's not part of the uniform.

GREENY: I've heard nine million reasons why managers wear uniforms. For example, it's because they have to go on the field. Does that mean that it would trip everyone up if Joe Torre makes a pitching change wearing a pair of khakis?

Another reason: Because there were player-managers historically, baseball managers wear uniforms today. Sure, if you're going to play and manage at the same time, go ahead and wear a uniform. I get it. Pete Rose playing and managing? Fine. In a uniform. Lou Piniella? Put on some normal clothes, for heaven's sakes!

Maybe Peter Gammons could shed some light on this. Peter, was there any good reason why the league was so adamant about checking Terry Francona's uniform during an actual game?

PETER GAMMONS: It was a disgrace, Greeny, and

someone should be fired over it. Terry Francona has a circulation problem, and he doesn't want to wear the uniform belt because of his illness. If you want to check him, do it before the game.

But the whole thing is silly to start with. If you want to talk about historical precedent—which is very popular these days—then consider Connie Mack. He did okay managing in a suit. But to be interrupting Francona when there's a runner on second base and they think he might steal—that just shows a total lack of understanding for the game.

GREENY: What do you think, Golic?

GOLIC: I think Peter Gammons should be the next commissioner of baseball.

GREENY: He'd make a great commissioner, for sure, but what about me?

GOLIC: *You* as the next commissioner?

GREENY: If I'm commissioner, Lou Piniella will be sitting in the dugout in a polo shirt, or maybe a nice cashmere sweater for the playoffs. It's just one of the changes I'd make if I was given the privilege of serving as the commissioner of baseball, which I hope to do one day. Seriously. M&M

GREENBERG
FOR COMMISSIONER

GOLIC: **Bud Selig's current contract as commissioner of Major League Baseball is set to expire after the 2012 season, at which time he plans to retire. The baseball owners will then have to gather and elect a new commish. My candidate for the job? Mike Greenberg!**

For as long as I've known him—which is too long—Greeny has dreamed about one day serving as baseball's commissioner. He keeps talking about it. A lot. He's even come up with a platform of 12 planks for his "12 for '12" campaign, which he is officially kicking off right here. So, is Greeny the right man for the job? To be perfectly honest with you, I have no idea. He could be awful. Who knows if he'll make the game any better or how much he'll ruin it. But at the very least, the geek will be off my hands. He'll be someone else's problem. I'll finally be rid of him and have my nice radio show back. And I'll be a very happy man again. So please, for the love of all things holy: VOTE FOR GREENY IN 2012!

GREENY'S "12 FOR '12" PLATFORM

I. The home run record is still 61

I'm determined to rid baseball of its steroid past and build a bridge to its clean future. So the next player to hit 62 or more home runs in a season will be the new home run king. Period. Let the shrapnel fall where it may on Bonds and McGwire and Sosa. What's more, the night the record is broken will make for great TV. We will test the player's urine—live on national television—immediately after he breaks 61. When the test comes back clean, I'll hold up the results and say, "Ladies and gentlemen, I present to you . . . the new home run champion!" The crowd will go nuts. Roger Maris's family will be on hand, and everyone will hug and cry. If the test comes back dirty, though, Maris will remain in the record books. And we might have to go to a commercial break.

II. More postseason baseball

It's more of an accomplishment to make the playoffs in baseball than it is in any other major professional sport. In the NFL, 37.5 percent of the teams get to the postseason, but only 26.7 percent of baseball teams make it. The teams that perform the best in the regular season should be given a greater chance to win in the playoffs, and it's much more likely for a fluke to affect the outcome of a five-game series than a seven-game series. I'll make the first round a best-of-seven series.

For those who'd argue that this would prolong the postseason, I will say this: It won't. The way the current schedule stands, the World Series begins in the middle of the week instead of the usual Saturday game. In other words, a handful of off-days are already built in. Adding two extra games—at most!—won't push anything back at all.

III. Stop moving the fences in

Home runs are great, but pitching duels are even better. I don't think baseball needs more 12–10 games—I like 3–2 games much more. But first I'll have to run this by my marketing people. I'll need a cabinet, of course, with a marketing czar, a department of defense, and secretary of beer concessions. I can't do all this by myself.

CHANGE

IV. Day games again

Baseball has finally returned to the idea of scheduling one game of the World Series as a day game. I've been talking about it for years to anyone who will listen: I'll make *every* weekend game in the postseason a day game. The games don't have to end in daylight; they simply have to start when it's still light outside. For games on the East Coast, this means a start time as late as 5:00 P.M. There's no earthly reason not to do it.

For those naysayers who want to accuse me of an East Coast bias: Would you rather have everyone see the beginning of a baseball game, or the end of one? If you gave anyone the choice of watching only the first three innings of a game or the last three innings, what fan would choose to see the start of the game knowing he won't be able to watch the end? You don't pick up a book and say, "I'll read the first 100 pages of this, and no matter how much I like it, I'm going to put it down. I won't read the rest." You don't walk out of a movie after an hour if you like it. Who does that?

V. A shorter season

I'm probably dating myself—it's okay, I dated myself all through high school—but I remember going to the ballpark as a kid in the middle of summer for an honest doubleheader. One gate, two games. And it was *great.* As commissioner, I'll bring back doubleheaders—every team will have at least one afternoon doubleheader per month in June, July, and August. The fans deserve this, and it would also help shorten the season so we won't have to worry about playing the World Series in the snow.

VI. Everyone plays by the same rules

On my very first day in office, I'll get rid of the designated hitter. I never liked the DH rule, and there's no reason why one league should play what is effectively a different game. If it means adding another spot on the roster to appease the players union, I don't have a problem with that.

VII. Franchises will no longer be coddled

Every state is represented in Congress, but not every team needs to be represented in the All-Star Game. The fans could have voted one of their players in, but they didn't. Whoever is managing the All-Star Game should be concerned with fielding the best team, not filling quotas. The All-Star Game isn't a democracy. It's a *game*.

VIII. No soup

For the most part, I applaud the culinary innovations that stadiums

have made in their concession menus. But selling soup at the ballpark? No way. Look, I like a good bowl of soup. I also like baseball. But soup and baseball just don't go together, and under no circumstances will I allow any major league ballpark to sell soup. You don't go to a baseball game and get soup. Never in my life have I heard anyone say, "Let's go to the ballpark and get a nice bowl of mushroom barley." It just doesn't work that way.

IX. 28 teams

As commissioner, I'll get rid of two teams. There's currently a glut of subpar players and bad pitchers in the league, and I'm seriously beginning to doubt whether some organizations will ever manage to field a competitive team. Baseball is a major sport, but with some franchises, you don't get the feeling that it is. They feel second-rate, and they have no business being in Major League Baseball. It's embarrassing.

I'm not going to relegate them to the minor leagues. I'll just get rid of them. Goodbye. We'll disburse their best players among the other teams and raise the quality of play in the league as a whole.

While I'm on it, they should subtract two teams in every major sport except the NFL—and four teams in the NBA. There are just too many lousy organizations. But I'm getting ahead of myself.

X. Everyone will have a roof over their heads, when needed . . .

Within three years, every ballpark will have its own retractable roof. How in the world can we continue to allow the weather to dictate whether games are going to be played, the conditions the games are played in, and the atmosphere for fans at the ballpark? How it will work is very simple: The roof will be open when conditions are pleasant, and it will be shut when they are not. Do we not have this technology, or am I missing something?

XI. And troughs for the men. Maybe.

The men's room at Wrigley Field has a long, two-sided trough with

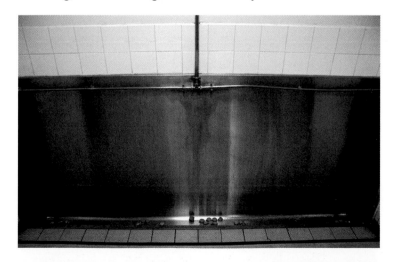

a partition in the middle that goes roughly up to your lower chest. In other words, you're face-to-face with your baseball-loving brethren while answering nature's call, experiencing a degree of brotherhood that can't be replicated anywhere else.

A baseball game is meant to bring people together. As commissioner, I'll immediately convene a blue-ribbon panel to explore the feasibility of implementing a trough-only policy for all of the men's bathrooms in our nation's ballparks.

XII. Seriously, leave RBIs alone

Nothing drives me crazier than a highfalutin sportscaster saying, "With 3 RBI last night, Albert Pujols now has 98 RBI for the season." What?

RBI is a word unto itself, and when you have more than one of

them, you make it plural. One RBI, two RBIs. Anyone who uses "RBI" as a plural noun is clearly deranged, and as commissioner I will not only ban them from every ballpark in the country, I'll forbid them from talking about baseball for one season. That's right: a gag order. It pains me to do this, but it pains me even more to hear "Two RBI." Makes my ears itch. "Runs batted in" is similar in construction to "prisoners of war." Walter Cronkite didn't say, "Five POW were released today."

There should be some things in life that you can count on. Like people saying "two RBIs." Or planets. There have always been nine of them in our solar system, but for some reason Pluto is suddenly not one of them— it's just another floating rock in space. That really bugs me. What's next, six dwarfs because Bashful no longer meets the criteria?

The point is that "RBIs" is something we've been saying since well before Pluto was a planet. When they first started playing baseball in the 19th century, someone said, "I had four RBIs today. It was a good day." That's the way it's always been. Stop messing with it.

RULE

2.96:

One Day, Athletes Will Rule the World.

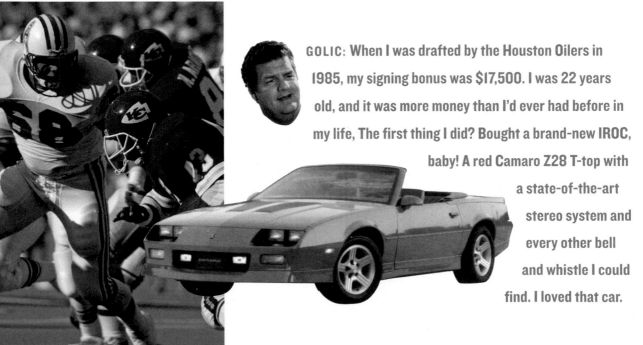

GOLIC: When I was drafted by the Houston Oilers in 1985, my signing bonus was $17,500. I was 22 years old, and it was more money than I'd ever had before in my life, The first thing I did? Bought a brand-new IROC, baby! A red Camaro Z28 T-top with a state-of-the-art stereo system and every other bell and whistle I could find. I loved that car.

Sure, I had jobs before. During summers after high school, I worked as a lifeguard at Manry Community Pool in my hometown of Willowick, Ohio. I think I made about $5 an hour, if that. The most lucrative job I had before pro football was back when I was 12 or 13, working with my brothers on side jobs for my dad, who was a bricklayer. I'd swing the sledge, break steps, chimneys, and driveways, haul debris, and do all the other dirty work. At the end of the day, Dad paid us in cash, $80 each, which was a healthy sum for a kid. But boy, did he work us. My dad was a tough boss, and God forbid he ever caught you sitting down.

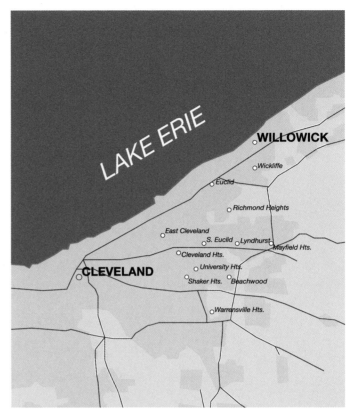

My starting salary in my rookie year was $62,000, and it felt like big money to me. I was single then, and my game checks went straight to my agent, who took care of all my bills—rent, electricity, credit card, telephone, everything. At nights I'd hit the bars with teammates and friends, give my credit card to the barkeep, and buy everyone drinks for the night. Never thought twice about it.

Three or four months later, the phone rings. It's my agent. "Listen, Mike," he says, "just because your credit card has a $5,000 limit doesn't mean you have to hit it every month." This was my first lesson in money management: Keep track of it. I was spending simply because I figured the money was there, and after a single two-minute phone call, I learned that I wasn't rich anymore, and never was.

In time I got better with the money, mostly because I married my wife. Chris had graduated from St. Mary's College with a degree in accounting, and she understood dollars and cents much better than I ever could. My job was to keep playing, and I did.

After Houston, I was picked up by the Eagles and, within a couple of years, I started making decent money. I even managed to secure a few endorsement deals, like with McDonald's and Chevrolet. I entered free agency coming off a pretty good season and was looking to cash in a little. I certainly wasn't high on their priority list—a good player, but not a great one—and the front office advised me to go out, find a deal, and then we'd talk. I visited a few other teams and quickly got an offer from Miami for two years at $700,000 and $750,000. I came back to the Eagles and asked for a little over $700,000.

They countered with $600,000.

I countered with, *Are you serious?*

They were. They explained to me that I could easily make up the difference with my endorsements, which didn't sound like an explanation at all. It sounded like BS—they should be paying me for my football and not worry about what I do off the field on my own time. But they wouldn't raise the offer, and it pissed me off. That year, their first-round draft pick was a kid out of Colorado who was a defensive tackle, which was my position. I figured that their plan was to start playing him and get rid of me, which pissed me off all the more. So I left. Signed with the Dolphins. Go with the one who loves you last.

As it happened, the guy the Eagles had drafted couldn't do anything and turned out to be a bust. Had I stayed, I probably would have gotten a lot of playing time. As for the Dolphins, I spent 10 years in Miami that one season. I tore my calf early and went from one injury to the next. My NFL career was soon over.

Looking back on it, I shouldn't have taken the negotiations with the Eagles as personally as I did. They were trying to get the best deal for them, and I was trying to get the best for me. That's all it was.

RULE 2.39

Athletes with multimillion-dollar contracts who complain about getting disrespected don't deserve your respect.

GREENY: People get down on athletes and their money. I'm not referring to your rookie-year signing bonus, which these days would be considered almost quaint. I'm also not referring to the other end of the spectrum, guys like Latrell Sprewell, who famously complained about a three-year, $21 million offer by saying, "I have a family to feed." Clearly, it was an absurd thing to say.

But consider someone like Reggie Bush, who was the second overall pick in the 2006 draft and sat out the start of training camp because he wanted first-pick money. In effect, Bush was holding out for a couple of million on a contract worth more than $25 million, and the fans let him have it. They resent players' salaries.

GOLIC: What I hear a lot of is, "I'd do it for free." No, you wouldn't. Sure, it was a great life, but I busted my ass for it. There's a lot of blood, sweat, tears, and puke that went into my career.

GREENY: As a fan, you have to stop and realize that professional athletes live in a completely different universe. Take football. It's late December, and you're playing a night game in Denver or Green Bay or Philly. It's six degrees outside, and you're out there with no sleeves on. *What?* What is wrong with you? Only in a crazy society would people think, "Boy, that guy is tough." If you saw some guy walking down the street on the coldest night of the year wearing a short-sleeved shirt, you'd say there's obviously something wrong with him. He's not tough, he's *insane.*

GOLIC: Yeah, you never played football.

GREENY: But that's my point—it's very easy to have an opinion about how you would do a job if you had it, until you actually have that job. That's a rule. It's easy for me to say that Reggie Bush should just shut up and take the $25 million. What's another $2 million? But that's not the way the world works.

The working definition of "rich" is "more money than I have." If I'm making $30,000, then the guy making $50,000 is rich. If I'm making $300,000, then the guy pulling down $500,000 is rich, and if it's $3 million, then $5 million is rich. When you're at that level, and you think you can get another $2 million, you'd do it. The fact that they're athletes getting paid to play a game is irrelevant. Someone is paying them to work.

GOLIC: I remember getting drafted and thinking, "This is going to be great, I'm in the pros, and it's going to be so much fun—I get to play and get paid for it." Then I show up, and it's, Be here at seven to lift, then a meeting at eight, then a walk-through, then lunch, another meeting, then practice, another meeting . . . and I'm thinking, "Jeez, this is an *actual job.*" It doesn't mean it can't be fun, though.

GREENY: Right, but when athletes complain that playing a sport is a job, look out. The Angels let Francisco Rodriguez—K-Rod, who holds the major league record for saves in a single season—walk away after seven years when they wouldn't match the kind of money that the Mets were sending his way. "It opens your eyes a little bit," K-Rod told Kevin Baxter of the *Los Angeles Times.* "Now you're not playing for the fun, you're playing for your career. Pretty much, you're an employee. . . . The day you don't get the job done, the day you get hurt, the day you don't do what they ask you to do, they'll throw you away and get someone else to do your job."

GOLIC: See, athletes like K-Rod are faced with a choice. If you really like it somewhere but staying means getting less money, then maybe stay for less money. Or leave. It's a decision that you have to make. With one year left on K-Rod's contract, the Angels offered him a three-year, $34 million deal, but he turned it down after the Yankees signed Mariano Rivera for three years at $45 million. Then the Angels signed

Torii Hunter for $90 million. K-Rod was looking for a five-year, $75 million deal, but the Angels didn't offer him that. He signed with the Mets for three years at $37 million. Because the negotiations with the Angels didn't work out for him, baseball isn't as much fun for him anymore. I get it.

GREENY: You want to know what the typical fan's reaction to that is? Where's Stats?

STATS: Tell him to cry himself to sleep with all his money. You play a game for a living, K-Rod. It's fun no matter where you play. You want my schedule for a week? Cry me a river, build a bridge, and get over it. You don't look too sad when you save a game and celebrate like a five-year-old getting a candy bar.

GREENY: Now *that's* a reaction from a fan who doesn't want to hear it.

GOLIC: That's the reaction of our angry young board operator, Mr. Negativity, who's 24 and too young to be so angry. What K-Rod said is *exactly* how it is. When you're playing in Little League or high school, it's pure fun. College is fun, too, but a little more businesslike. In the pros, it's all business, and you *are* an employee. At times, you have to find ways to get up for it, but it's difficult. One of the lines you always hear the older players say is, "Remember when you were young and playing just for the fun of it. Get that feeling back." Everyone goes through it.

GREENY: Look, I don't begrudge any of these guys getting every penny they can. But when they say it isn't as fun as it used to be, guess what? Being an accountant or a stockbroker isn't fun like Little League baseball. Driving a cab isn't, either. You've got a job, and it feels like a job? News flash! They're not giving you $50 million or $5 million or $500,000 to have fun. You can sit at home and read a book all day, but no one's going to pay you millions of dollars to do it.

GOLIC: I completely disagree with you, because most people don't think pro athletes have a job. They think they're playing a game and having fun. But you're playing the game all your life, doing nothing different from what you were doing as a kid. What did you do in Pee Wee Football? Stop the run and get to the quarterback. High school? Stop the run and get to the quarterback. College? Stop the run and get to the quarterback. The pros? Stop the run and get to the quarterback. It's the same thing, over and over again.

GREENY: I remember when I was living in Chicago and first wanted to get into radio. I used to get up every morning and read the *Chicago Tribune* out loud like it was a sportscast. I'd sit there by myself at the kitchen table and read aloud Jerome Holtzman and Mike Royko. It's really not all that different from what I'm doing now, but it's most definitely not the same. They don't call it "work" because it has a nice ring to it. It's *work*. And if you didn't see that coming, don't call the fan the fool.

But not all sports are created equal. Remember when Mark Spitz came on the show just before the Beijing Games? Here is an incredible athlete who had won seven gold medals in Munich in 1972, something no one had ever done

in the history of the Olympics until Michael Phelps came along. And now? He showed up and started pitching Botox.

GOLIC: I've got no problem with Spitz selling Botox, and I've got no problem with Michael Phelps cashing in right away and never having to work another day in his life. That's the reality of today's market. If you can make a living with endorsement deals and speeches, why not? Believe me, a lot of Olympic athletes would love to be like Mark Spitz and milk the gold for as long as possible. And if you can make $20 million at it right off the bat, you'd be as happy as a pig in slop.

GREENY: Look, you can't make much money as a professional swimmer. I mean *none.* For most Olympic athletes who win gold, they try to get endorsements, do commercials, make talk show appearances, and, if they're lucky, give speeches, write books, get into movies, and walk the red carpet as often and as long as they possibly can. But then there's a guy like Eric Heiden, who won five individual gold medals in speed skating at Lake Placid. An amazing accomplishment, but where is Eric Heiden these days? Not on the red carpet. He's an orthopedic surgeon out west.

RULE 2.44

Every amateur athlete should aspire to become a professional celebrity.

GOLIC: If Eric Heiden was in a movie, I'd go see it, but I don't know if I'd go out of my way to have him perform any kind of surgery on me. You want the guy who's been doing nothing his whole life except studying. A complete geek, not some famous guy.

GREENY: Actually, I understand that Eric Heiden is a world-class surgeon, both a jock *and* a geek.

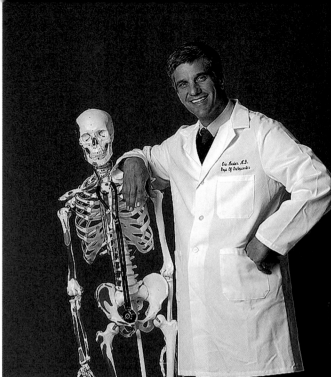

GOLIC: Then he's the exception that proves the rule. I once heard that Mark Spitz went on to become a dentist in California, but that turned out not to be true. Thank God. He was actually selling real estate. Spitz doing my root canal? No thanks. His hands might still be wet from a swim. The drill could slip from his hand.

GREENY: If Mark Spitz comes anywhere near me with so much as a piece of dental floss, I'm running in the other direction. Here's my idea for Spitz and Phelps and every Olympic swimmer out there, not that they asked. Four words, my friend: *Swimming with the Stars.*

Look at *Dancing with the Stars.* I mean, who really thought that would do well? We'll do *Swimming with the Stars.* You have Phelps and Spitz and a bunch of other swimmers, and they'll race with celebrities. You get famous people who look good in bathing suits, and believe me, people are going to watch. Men and women.

RULE 2.45

Beware Olympic heroes bearing dental equipment.

It's minor surgery on the other guy.

MARK "STINK" SCHLERETH: During my 12 years in the NFL, I went under the knife 29 times. Twenty of those surgeries were on my knees. I've had scopes done, ligaments sewn up, microfractures fused, you name it. I dreaded it every single time. The medical staff always reminds you about the inherent risks—infections, amputations, sometimes even death. You never know. Minor surgery? When they're wheeling you into that operating room, it's never minor for you.

After the surgery, there's always the recovery and physical therapy, but the hardest thing you'll confront as an athlete is the fact that you will never be the same again.

Sure, the doctors will tell you that the surgery was a success, but what else are they going to say? "Boy, did I screw that one up!" You're altered, and your body will never work exactly right. Nobody tells you that, and nobody will tell you how mentally tough it's going to be to trust your body enough to get back out there. It will take a bigger leap of faith than you ever imagined. You will feel not quite there yet, but if you wait, you'll not-quite-there yourself out of the sport.

swimming
with the **stars**

GOLIC: You wouldn't even have to get A-listers. *Dancing with the Stars* does fine without them. You can get plenty of B- and C-listers looking to get back into the limelight. Somebody like Paris Hilton would do it.

GREENY: I wonder what David Souter is up to these days. You'd team up the famous people with great swimmers, and then they'd train together during the week, just like *Dancing with the Stars*. And then you have them swim. They'd do a relay race: Tom Wopat or John Schneider jumps in and does a lap, and then Michael Phelps does a lap. Couldn't you picture this?

GOLIC: I'd do it.

GREENY: Good idea. We'll get some gutsy ones who look terrible in bathing suits, like you. That would be funny.

RULE 2.48: The biggest losers always wind up as the biggest winners.

GOLIC: There's hope for you yet, Greeny.

GREENY: This rule is about professional athletes. It's sad, but I think it's true. Here's why: The better you are, the more home runs you hit or touchdowns you score, the more a team will put up with behavior that in any other line of work would get you fired. Take Chad Johnson. Eight hours before kickoff against the Steelers a couple of years ago, Johnson walked into a team meeting late, leaned his head against the wall, and closed his eyes. He was told to pay attention. Instead, Johnson stood up, left the room, and got into a heated argument with the head coach.

Did they get rid of him? Yes and no. The team deactivated him for the game. In other words, the Bengals paid him to go away.

I've never played in the NFL, but I don't think anyone can argue that it's okay to be falling asleep in a meeting of any kind. Who would think that's anything but extremely disrespectful?

GOLIC: Basically he was saying *I don't care.* But you know, when the Bengals deactivated him, he'd played in every single game for them since Week 10 of the 2001 season—that's 113 consecutive games. He's controversial, but he's also an excellent receiver.

RULE 2.49(a)

Never give yourself a nickname.

Our television cameraman is Ubaldo (né Dan Filipone). ESPN Radio's program manager is The Gnome (né Scott Shapiro). Our associate producer is Joaquin, which most people don't realize isn't his real name until it's too late (Curt Kaplan, but we didn't tell you that).

He almost wasn't Joaquin, though. For years, he was just Curt, and one day he told us that he wanted a nickname, and he wanted it to be T-Bone. Why T-Bone? "No reason," Curt explained. "I've just always wanted to be called T-Bone." No way, we told him. You *can't* give yourself a nickname. It just doesn't work that way. So we came up with our own candidate—Joaquin, after Kelly Ripa's son, because at the time we were going through a heavy Kelly Ripa infatuation—and left it up to our radio audience to decide: Joaquin or T-Bone? Joaquin won by a landslide, and that was that.

GREENY: That's my point. Chad Johnson wins. Either the Bengals will pay him a whole bunch of money, or someone else will. Keyshawn Johnson won in Tampa Bay. Same with Terrell Owens wherever he plays. No matter what they do or how poorly they behave, they'll eventually get their way. It's that simple.

GOLIC: We're seeing NFL coaches try to take more of a stand now, certainly more than in my day. Remember when the Panthers suspended Steve Smith? In Jacksonville, Jack Del Rio took Mike Peterson, the defensive *captain,* and sent him home two days in a row. These are major guys.

GREENY: But who thinks it's acceptable in any work environment to walk into a meeting late and fall asleep? I don't care where you work—it's thoroughly

RULE 2.49(b)

Fine, don't listen to us. But if you give yourself a nickname, at least make sure it makes sense in Spanish, Mr. *Ochenta Cinco*.

disrespectful to the person running the meeting, to the other people who are sitting there and paying attention, and to the person who's ultimately paying you to be at that meeting. It just boggles the mind that anyone might think that's okay. Who can defend that?

GOLIC: I'm not defending it, but he's not the first player to fall asleep at a team meeting, and he won't be the last. I've dozed off my fair share.

GREENY: You have?

GOLIC: Oh, yeah. When the room's dark and I'm tired, I'd nod off occasionally, sure. Especially if it was after a tough practice or early in the morning. Players sometimes fall asleep at meetings.

GREENY: Really? And what happened when the coach saw you sleeping?

GOLIC: Never got caught.

GREENY: See, this is a great example of how you accept some things in sports as a given, and the rest of us are thinking, *What?*

GOLIC: Are you kidding me? You don't think anyone's ever nodded off in a conference room with 40 other people there and a PowerPoint presentation with the lights off?

GREENY: Maybe, but they'd get fired. Or it's something that's so rare, it happened 10 years ago and everyone's still talking about how Phil in accounting got canned because he fell asleep. Mike, I've got to tell you, people in normal jobs don't fall asleep in meetings.

GOLIC: I'm not saying they're lying on the floor and snoring. Just dozing off now and again.

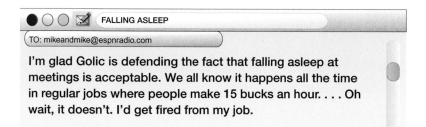

I'm glad Golic is defending the fact that falling asleep at meetings is acceptable. We all know it happens all the time in regular jobs where people make 15 bucks an hour. . . . Oh wait, it doesn't. I'd get fired from my job.

GOLIC: I never said it was acceptable! I said I did it, and I said that coaches aren't happy if you do. You'll get yelled at. But there's no way you can tell me it never happens in the real world.

GREENY: I've been working in the real world for 20 years, and I'm telling you that if you fell asleep, it would be a very big deal.

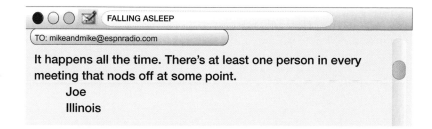

It happens all the time. There's at least one person in every meeting that nods off at some point.
    Joe
    Illinois

GREENY: Great. Does Joe work in a sleep apnea clinic?

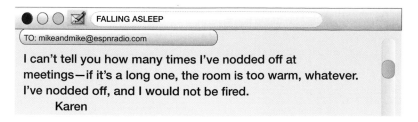

I can't tell you how many times I've nodded off at meetings—if it's a long one, the room is too warm, whatever. I've nodded off, and I would not be fired.
    Karen

GOLIC: So many e-mails are backing me up on this one.

GREENY: Okay, maybe I'm wrong. Maybe the entire world is falling asleep at meetings and I don't know about it. It seems to me that if you're running a serious place of business, if you're serious about what you're trying to accomplish, then you don't have people falling asleep at meetings. Why have meetings in the first place if they're sleeping? What's the point?

And this happens all the time in the NFL? Somebody wake up Ron Jaworski and ask him what he knows.

RON JAWORSKI: Well, Greeny, I've never fallen asleep at a meeting, but I'll admit there were times I closed my eyes and drifted off a little. Golic's probably more familiar with this, but in our era we used to have these Kodak projectors, so you had to have the lights off. The room was dark. Always.

GOLIC: Right, and the projectors had those little fans in them that would make the perfect white noise. You'd wind up helpless with your head banging off the desk.

RON JAWORSKI: Guys would get to meetings early so they could get one of the back seats, lean their head against the wall, and nod off. And I've got to be honest about this—I've woken up *coaches* at meetings. It was during Dick

Vermeil's time, when the coaching staff was getting maybe two or three hours of sleep a night. Some of them would look forward to the meetings because it meant they could catch a little shut-eye.

GOLIC: Great, Jaws. Thanks. So what do you think now, Greeny?

GREENY: If I'm wrong, I'm wrong. I stand corrected, but I'll stay awake while I do it. I've got to tell you that none of this makes any sense to me. I'm in a state of shock. I'm discovering that we live in a much sleepier country than I thought.

RULE 2.53: If you think all athletes are spoiled brats, remind yourself of J. P. Hayes.

GREENY: Never heard of J. P. Hayes? You're not alone. Although he's been a pro golfer for 20 years and has won a couple of PGA tournaments, he's not a household name by any means. Even those who follow the Tour closely would have a hard time picking him out of a lineup. But after we read a short news story on the air about Hayes's remarkable—some would say extraordinary—decision, our inbox exploded with messages of praise, disbelief, disagreement, and even a confession.

In late 2008, Hayes was trying to earn his PGA card at a second-stage qualifier in McKinney, Texas. He was halfway to Q-School, where only the top 25 finishers make it to the pro tour. The pressure at the qualifiers is intense, and so is the competition. Hayes was playing well and was about to tee off on the 12th hole when he asked his caddy for a new ball. It was then that his

RULE **2.54**

Whenever someone says, "I'm being completely honest," they might as well be telling you they go to Hooters for the wings.

GOLIC: Boy, I sure love the wings at Hooters.

GREENY: Nobody goes to Hooters for the wings.

GOLIC: I do. When the boys were growing up—we were living in Orlando, I had just retired from the Dolphins, the kids were young—we'd go to Hooters.

GREENY: You took your *kids* to Hooters?

GOLIC: For the wings. We all went. It's not like I said, "Hey, c'mon, boys, I'm going to show you what women look like." I'm tellin' you, I love the wings. So one time we're sitting there—me, my wife, my sons, Mike and Jake—and Mike starts staring at a waitress who's standing right in front of him. He's looking at her from head to toe. I mean, he's four years old, and he's checking her out. The waitress looks over, looks at me, and says, "Four-year-olds can get away with that."

GREENY: Wait, what did she mean, *get away with that*?

GOLIC: Right. They're wearing those outfits, and they don't expect anyone to look?

GREENY: Here's the thing: Women wear something incredibly revealing, and if a man looks at them, they say, "What are you looking at?" What the hell do you mean, what am I looking at? Go put on a suit of armor if you don't want me looking. You're dressing that way to attract exactly the kind of attention that you're now falsely pretending offends you. This bothers me. Now, I have total respect for people who are waitresses at Hooters, but if you're going to be a waitress at Hooters, what do you think people are there for? They're *not* coming in for the wings.

GOLIC: Except for me.

caddy made a terrible mistake—he pulled a different type of ball than the one Hayes had been using before, a clear violation of the tournament rules. By the time Hayes noticed the difference, it was too late—he had already hit the ball into play. As soon as he realized it, he called over an official, explained what had happened, and was assessed a two-shot penalty. This was bad, but it wasn't the end of the world for him. He finished the round with a 74 and shot a 71 the next day, and was still in a very good position to advance to the next qualifying stage.

But then Hayes made a shocking discovery. Alone in his hotel room the night before the third round, he looked into his golf bag and realized that the ball his caddy had given him the other day wasn't just a different model Titleist. It was actually a prototype ball, unapproved and most likely illegal. What did Hayes do about it? "I called an official in Houston that night and said, 'I think I may have a problem,' " Hayes later told Gary D'Amato of the *Milwaukee Journal Sentinel.* "He said they'd call Titleist the next day. I pretty much knew at that point I was going to be disqualified." Indeed, he was disqualified—from the tournament in Texas, from Q-School, and from playing in any PGA event for the next 12 months. What's more, he didn't consider what he had done to be all that out of the ordinary. After his self-inflicted disqualification, Hayes said, "Everybody out here would have done the same thing."

Would you?

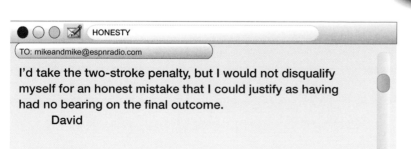

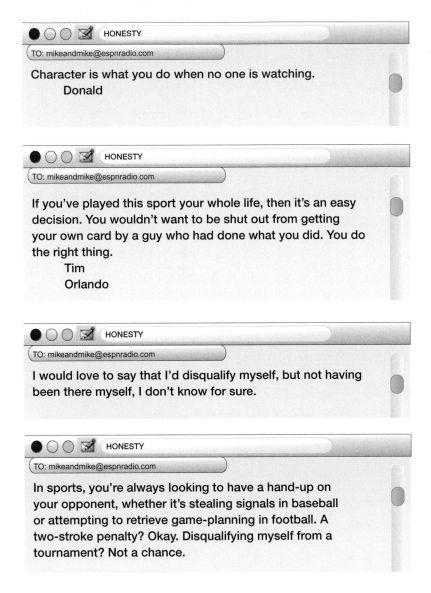

HONESTY

TO: mikeandmike@espnradio.com

Character is what you do when no one is watching.
Donald

HONESTY

TO: mikeandmike@espnradio.com

If you've played this sport your whole life, then it's an easy decision. You wouldn't want to be shut out from getting your own card by a guy who had done what you did. You do the right thing.
Tim
Orlando

HONESTY

TO: mikeandmike@espnradio.com

I would love to say that I'd disqualify myself, but not having been there myself, I don't know for sure.

HONESTY

TO: mikeandmike@espnradio.com

In sports, you're always looking to have a hand-up on your opponent, whether it's stealing signals in baseball or attempting to retrieve game-planning in football. A two-stroke penalty? Okay. Disqualifying myself from a tournament? Not a chance.

GREENY: You know the song "Honesty" by Billy Joel? "Everyone is so untrue." Well, not everyone. Not J. P. Hayes. It's one thing to take a two-stroke penalty, but it's another matter entirely when you're completely alone in your hotel room and you're the only one in the entire world who will ever know what happened.

Hayes has made a very good living for himself with golf, earning $7 million throughout his years on the tour, so going a year without a card doesn't mean he's out on the street and his children are starving. Yet he could have made a significantly *better* living had he not said a word. Getting a PGA card is as big a deal as it can possibly get for this guy. This is how he makes his living. This is his life. One shot during one hole in one round—there's zero chance that anyone would have ever called him on it, and he could have just kept his mouth shut. But he didn't, and that's amazing.

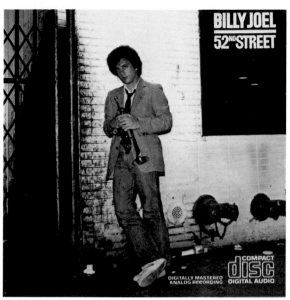

GOLIC: Without a doubt what he did was commendable, but let's keep in mind that this is golf, a sport that has a very specific rule about calling penalties on yourself. There are no officials watching your every move, so it's expected that if you do something against the rules—big or small, anything—you turn yourself in. A lot of people would say that they expect that kind of behavior from athletes in all sports, but that's going too far.

GREENY: So honesty is more important than money when you're swinging a golf club, but not so much when you're shooting a free throw?

GOLIC: Both my sons played high school football. Mike, Jr. played center, and Jake was a tight end. Let's say that during a game Jake trapped a ball, but the official didn't see it hit the ground and ruled it a catch. Was Jake supposed to go over to the referee and tell him he didn't catch it? If I was Jake's coach, what was I supposed to tell him? "Jake, you trapped the ball. If that happens again, I want you to go over to the official and tell him that you didn't catch it." Not a chance! It's not what you do in football. Nor should it be. You sell it as a catch. Sports like football and baseball are about pushing the envelope, and players try to bend the rules—or even break them—if it means that it will benefit the team. If I can get away with something that helps me get to the quarterback, then I'm gonna do it. You find the corners, and you work them. Every player knows where the lines are. I bent the rules, and the people I played against did the exact same thing. How's that for honesty? If you want to call me an idiot, go ahead, because then every football player out there is an idiot, too. It's the culture of the sport, and the culture of golf is very different from the culture of football, or baseball, or basketball.

GREENY: What about the culture of life? What does that tell you to do?

GOLIC: I love football, Greeny, but it's *football,* okay? It's not life. You have officials on the field who police the game. In golf, you're the player, but you're also the referee. I can't think of another professional sport where the athletes police themselves to the extent that they do in golf. It's what makes the sport unique—and that includes tennis, because on the professional level there are officials on the court making the calls, not like in high school where you're making your own calls. If you're going to be your own referee, then you as a player are expected to conduct yourself with integrity and honesty. In sports where you have athletes playing the game and referees policing them, the rules of conduct are different. And that's the same as in life. If I'm going 75 miles an hour and I pass a police car on the side of the road and he doesn't stop me, am I supposed to turn around and tell him to give me a speeding ticket? Get real.

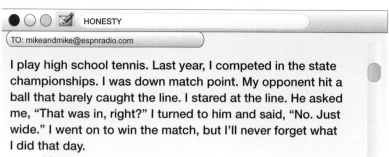

HONESTY

TO: mikeandmike@espnradio.com

I play high school tennis. Last year, I competed in the state championships. I was down match point. My opponent hit a ball that barely caught the line. I stared at the line. He asked me, "That was in, right?" I turned to him and said, "No. Just wide." I went on to win the match, but I'll never forget what I did that day.
    Matt
    Oklahoma

GREENY: Wow, that was an interesting email. At least Matt now realizes what he did was wrong.

Look, I'm not going to argue that all golfers are choirboys. They're not. If cheating is going on in golf—and nothing tells me that it's not—then we simply don't know about it.

But what about the idea of sportsmanship? You're playing football, but not in Veterans Stadium. It's in your backyard. A friendly game. And let's say—just for the sake of argument here, because I realize you're very fat and no one in his right mind would want you doing this—but let's say you ran out for a pass and trapped the ball. Would you say something?

GOLIC: Yeah, I probably would. And if I'm playing golf with a foursome for a $20 Nassau, and I hit the ball off the fairway and it lands dead behind a tree, I'm not going to move the ball. Why? Because that's how golf is meant to be played.

GREENY: Well, you're out 20 bucks. It's not going to change your life. But what if you discovered that your bank made an error and deposited an extra

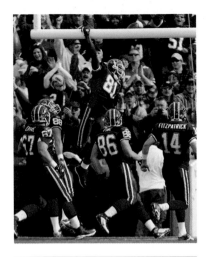

TOUCHDOWN! NOW WHAT?

RULE: It's okay to act like you've never been there before. And never will be again.

RULE: Go ahead and spike the football. Just make sure you're in the end zone first.

RULE: Use props at your own peril.

RULE: No taunting.

RULE: Your rival's celebrations are always dumb and annoying.

$50,000 into your account by mistake. Would you tell them? Or let's say you're at a department store and the person behind the register rings you up, but it's wrong—it's a few hundred dollars less than it should be. Would you say something?

GOLIC: In the financial situation I am in now, I'd probably tell them. But what if you're going through some tough times. You're behind in your mortgage, barely living paycheck to paycheck, and you've got three kids. They really need coats for the winter. Now, you might not feel good about your decision, but I can see how someone could rationalize it. The bank or the department store has lots of money; you don't. So you're going to try to get away with this one. We all hear stories about people who have nothing and find a bag of money and turn it in to the police. That's unbelievably commendable. But would I think less of them if they took the money and didn't say anything? Tough to say.

GREENY: Okay. Same person, walking down the street. Lost his job. Broke. Can't pay the rent. Sees an envelope fall out of an elderly woman's pocketbook, picks it up and sees that it's $500 in cash. Give it back to the old lady? And if not, is that person stealing?

GOLIC: Wow. I'm not saying that everyone who's financially strained would or should take it, but that's a tough, tough call.

GREENY: There are all sorts of gray areas here, but there's one aspect of honesty that's very cut-and-dry, and one profession that is consistently and clearly out-of-bounds. And we're going to get into a confrontation over it.

GOLIC: You and me?

GREENY: No, not the two of us. We're going to stand united in this.

GOLIC: We are?

GREENY: Yes, we are. Let's say the Saints are playing the Bears at Soldier Field late in the season, and the weatherman is saying that a blizzard is going to hit Chicago around the time of the game. Should you care?

GOLIC: No, not at all, because chances are I'll turn on the TV on Sunday, and do you know what I'll be able to see? The game. Very clearly.

GREENY: Right. No blizzard. No snow. None.

RULE 2.61: The weatherman is lying to you.

GREENY: It's time someone got tough with the Al Rokers and Sam Champions of the world. They've been able to make a fortune just by guessing. Sure, they all talk about their fancy equipment, their Doppler 3000 or whatever it's called, but have you ever seen a Doppler 3000? You haven't, because there's no such thing. It's a complete myth.

GOLIC: And those colors on the maps don't mean anything, either. They're just nice little gadgets to take your focus away from the fact that the weatherman doesn't know what he's talking about.

GREENY: Whenever we expose the myth of the weatherman, people get upset. And they send us e-mail. Like Mark, a meteorologist from Washington, D.C.—or so he says. We have no way of knowing that for sure. It's our word against his, but let's just say that he is.

WEATHER

TO: mikeandmike@espnradio.com

Greeny,
Let me get this straight. The sports talk host who picks football games as the Stone Cold Lead Pipe Locks and gets them wrong is criticizing the weatherman?

Forecasting the weather is very much like predicting the outcomes of sporting events. You process and analyze all the information you can find, and then make an educated decision based on that. Here's a challenge: I'll forecast the weather for an upcoming Sunday in Chicago, and you predict the final score of the Bears game. Let's see who's closer.
Mark

GOLIC: He's comparing what he does as a meteorologist to what we do when we predict the outcomes of football games?

GREENY: When we make our picks, we don't pretend to know what will happen. But not so with the weatherman. The evening news programs are always teasing the weather with, "After the break: Don't miss the forecast!" If they were honest about it, they'd say, "Up next, Biff Scott will take a guess on what the weather might be like during your morning commute." But they don't say that, because nobody would watch.

The problem with the weatherman is that he tells you he knows what the weather will be. He says, This is going to be the weather. But no one in their right mind goes on the air and says they know with certainty what the outcome of a football game will be. No one pretends to know.

GOLIC: The players don't know. The coaches don't know. Sports talk radio hosts don't know.

GREENY: But the weatherman pretends to know.

GOLIC: And what's amazing is when two different meteorologists on different channels in the same city give you two different forecasts.

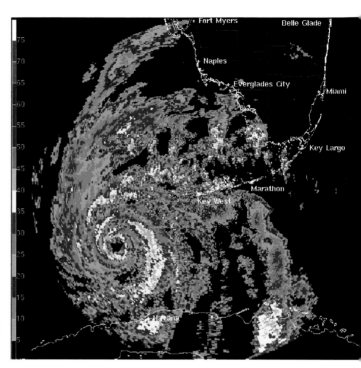

GREENY: Right. Is the Doppler 3000 in one studio not the same as the Doppler 3000 in the other studio? Are they using different machinery? Is any of this based on actual data?

We are *guessing* when we make our football picks. And did Mark admit in his e-mail that he's guessing, too? They can try to dazzle us with their high-tech toys, but it's all just fancy talk about nothing. We're on to you, weatherman, and we'll stay on until you own up to the truth.

GOLIC: Wow. You know, the last time I saw you this excited was the day you came into work with a new man-bag.

GREENY: I've been trashing weathermen since I was a sports anchor for CLTV in Chicago. My reports would always get shortened because of the weatherman. Storm coming? Sorry, Greeny, you're losing 20 seconds. Heat wave? Thirty seconds gone. But the storm never came, or it was sunny and pleasant with little humidity. Obviously, this was all just the weatherman's ploy to get more airtime.

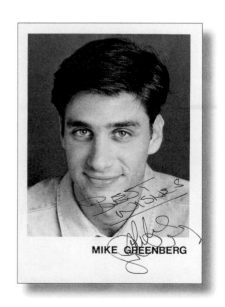

MIKE GREENBERG

GOLIC: Yeah, they were messing with the wrong guy.

GREENY: You know, athletes talk trash all the time, but every so often it escalates to the point where it crosses a line it clearly shouldn't. Before the Steelers played the Ravens in Week 4 of the 2008 season, the team's first-round draft pick, running back Rashard Mendenhall, sent a text message to a friend on the Ravens, saying he was going to have a big game against them. It was Mendenhall's first career start—no doubt he was excited—but the Ravens defense took note of his boast. On the first play from scrimmage at the start of the second half, Mendenhall took the handoff and was absolutely crushed by Ray Lewis. The hit broke Mendenhall's shoulder blade; he left the field and did not return.

During a radio interview following the game, Ravens defensive end Terrell Suggs was asked if the team had a bounty on Mendenhall. "The bounty was out on him," Suggs answered flatly, "and the bounty was out on 86 [Steelers wide receiver Hines Ward]. We just didn't get him between the whistles." Later, Ray Lewis told Dan Patrick that the force of the hit was "freakin' incredible. . . . After the play, I wasn't screaming, 'He's hurt!' I was screaming, 'He's done!' "

Indeed, Mendenhall was done—he would miss the rest of the season, and Lewis knew that before he sat down for his interview with Patrick.

The Steelers' head coach, Mike Tomlin, didn't make a big deal out of Suggs's or Lewis's comments, and neither did one of their intended targets, Hines Ward. "Baltimore, the bounties . . . I'll worry about that later," Ward said after hearing about Suggs's vendetta.

"Everyone in our division, I'm pretty sure they all have a bounty on me. . . . Everybody wants to knock this smile off my face."

But all of this, especially because the kid was a rookie and was knocked out for the year, really rubbed me the wrong way. As a fan—I never played the game. But you have, so I'm curious to know what you think.

GOLIC: Are bounties real? *Yes.* Were they around when I played? *Yes.* Did the teams I played with have bounties out on specific players? *Yes.*

GREENY: But what does "bounty" mean, exactly? You earn something if the guy doesn't finish the season?

GOLIC: Doesn't finish the game. You don't care about the season. Usually it starts with the team sitting around the meeting room. Someone might say, "A hundred bucks if Steve Young doesn't finish." Somebody else might kick in another hundred, and a few others will throw some more money into the pot. Soon you're up to $500. Now, it doesn't mean that you're going to pull Steve Young's leg out of the socket when he's down or try to snap his arm in a pileup. But if you hit him hard and he has to leave the game—a clean, legal hit—you get the cash.

Was the bounty going to affect the way I played against the 49ers or Steve Young? Not one bit. And whether or not there was a bounty out on Rashard Mendenhall, it had absolutely no effect on Ray Lewis, either—he was going to deliver that hit regardless. It was a devastating collision, but it was also as clean as could be, and it was going to break his shoulder. It had nothing to do with a bounty.

STEP **1.**
READ CAREFULLY.

STEP **2.**
TAPE PAGE TO INSIDE
OF LOCKER.

"I never even knew that was in the rulebook."

The words are Donovan McNabb's, spoken after neither the Philadelphia Eagles nor the Cincinnati Bengals could manage a score in the extra overtime period of their regular season game. As the official NFL rulebook states, if neither team scores, the game ends in a tie. Donovan didn't know.

Here at *Mike and Mike*, we're nothing if not interested in public service. We're here to help. Actually, we'll let Joaquin help you.

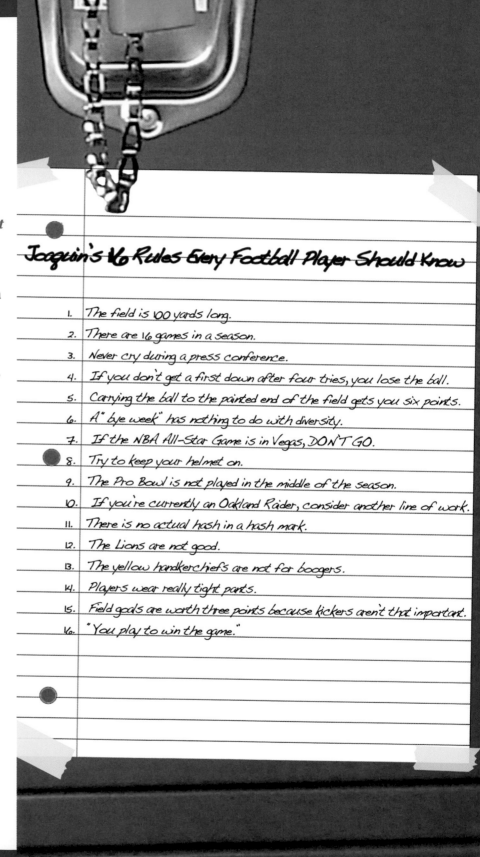

Joaquin's ~~No~~ 16 Rules Every Football Player Should Know

1. The field is 100 yards long.
2. There are 16 games in a season.
3. Never cry during a press conference.
4. If you don't get a first down after four tries, you lose the ball.
5. Carrying the ball to the painted end of the field gets you six points.
6. A "bye week" has nothing to do with diversity.
7. If the NBA All-Star Game is in Vegas, DON'T GO.
8. Try to keep your helmet on.
9. The Pro Bowl is not played in the middle of the season.
10. If you're currently an Oakland Raider, consider another line of work.
11. There is no actual hash in a hash mark.
12. The Lions are not good.
13. The yellow handkerchiefs are not for boogers.
14. Players wear really tight pants.
15. Field goals are worth three points because kickers aren't that important.
16. "You play to win the game."

GREENY: **Then why have it or talk about it? I don't get it.**

GOLIC: **It's just one of those things that happens. A macho thing. Pride. No one's thinking, "I'm gonna hurt this guy so I can get $500." It's just locker room talk.**

GREENY: **If it's talk that's only for the locker room, why does everyone else hear it, too? One of the most notorious games in NFL history is Buddy Ryan's Bounty Bowl, the Eagles versus the Cowboys on Thanksgiving Day, 1989. You actually played in it.**

GOLIC: **But the Bounty Bowl was not about money. Buddy was just pissed off at the kicker, Luis Zendejas. After Zendejas got cut from the Eagles, he shot his mouth off a little, and Buddy didn't appreciate it. He was looking to get even with him, and he sent a rookie out on a kickoff and told him to hit the kicker. Normally, you leave the kicker alone because he's not athletic enough to get downfield and make the tackle—if your returner finds himself one-on-one with the kicker and gets brought down, he's going to hear about it in meetings the next day.**

But on that play, we just chose to block the kicker, and the rookie hit Zendejas. I mean, he *smoked* him. The refs didn't throw a flag on the play because it was a perfectly legal block. No money changed hands, either.

We did have a little something on Ricky Watters and Steve Young at one time. And I'm sure Ron Jaworski can tell you how the Eagles gave out other rewards for big hits or for knocking someone out of a game—sometimes it was fishing poles, sometimes a color TV.

GREENY: Wait a sec. Is this a football game or a game show? *You just took Roger Staubach out at the knees! Come on down!*

GOLIC: It wasn't **HD**, though. Probably a set with rabbit ears.

GREENY: And this happens throughout the league?

GOLIC: I can't say that for sure, but it wouldn't surprise me, and it wouldn't bother me, either.

GREENY: Bounties, as a rule, don't sound right. But let's toss this up to someone who also has years of **NFL** experience, ESPN's very own Mark Schlereth. Stink?

STINK: **All this talk about bounties doesn't rub me the right way either, Greeny. It's a lot of bravado, but it's also silly. It doesn't reflect well on the league.**

GREENY: On the teams you played with, did they have bounties?

STINK: **I've never been around talk of $500 to knock somebody out of a game. We'd say that if you cut the guy before the 20-yard line on a kickoff, you might get $100 or $500 or whatever.**

GREENY: Which to me is very different than a bounty.

A good story makes for a great nickname.

 GOLIC: Like Mark Schlereth's—"Stink."

MARK "STINK" SCHLERETH: A lot of people think the reason I'm called Stink is because I used to wet my pants all the time when I was playing in the NFL. There aren't any bathrooms on the sidelines, and it would have taken me too long to hobble over to the tunnel and into the locker room. The fewer steps I took on my bad knees, the better. I didn't pee in my pants during a game—I peed in my pants during *every* game. But that's not the reason I'm called Stink.

During my rookie season with the Washington Redskins, my sister was teaching in an Eskimo village in Alaska called Akiachak, population 585. She told me how the villagers would catch the first run of salmon, cut the heads off, bury them, and then six weeks later dig up the rotted fish heads and eat them. They called them "stinkheads," and my sister said the whole town reeked of rotten fish. So of course I told my teammates the story of the Eskimo village of Akiachak and the stinkheads while we were eating lunch one day. From that point forward, I became Stinkhead and eventually just Stink, even though I was from Anchorage and not the Eskimo village of Akiachak.

STINK: It is, but it wouldn't bother me if a player said that he's got a bounty out on some clown and he's going to get very physical with him. That's very different than saying you're going to maliciously try to hurt someone.

GOLIC: Are you saying there's something wrong with having bounties or with talking about them publicly?

WHEN WE COME BACK ON PAGE 76, WE'LL DISCUSS THE DIRTIEST LITTLE SECRET IN THE NFL.

THE MIKE AND MIKE PENTATHLON

GREENY: When my kids asked me to run in a 5K charity race to help raise money for their school, I said yes. Whenever I say yes to anything, I always mean no.

I'm not much of an athlete. I'm not much of a runner, either. My wife can tell you that I'm not much of anything at all. There would be other parents at the race, and children, too. I didn't want to embarrass anyone, especially me, so I laced up a pair of sneakers and started training. My goal? To run the 5K—about 3.1 miles—in 24 minutes, which works out to a pace of eight minutes per mile. Far from world-class, but nothing to be ashamed of for a 40-year-old man.

Soon it was race day. Stretching out before the starting gun, I see my friend Jon, who has also entered the 5K and is a very good runner. We start the race, and I settle into a nice little trot. I notice that Jon has not passed me. This is good, I tell myself, and I come up with a strategy for the race: Stay ahead of Jon.

About a mile in, Jon pulls up and is now running alongside me. I make a slight adjustment to my original racing strategy: Stay with Jon.

So I'm staying with Jon and I'm running, running, running. A few minutes later I make another racing adjustment: Stay close to Jon.

At the two-mile mark: Keep Jon within my sights.

Finally, near the end of the race, a new plan entirely: Remember what color shirt Jon's wearing. Because by this point, he's running with the lead pack far, far ahead, wherever that may be. I decide that Jon was probably wearing blue.

I was hurting and experiencing major cardiovascular pain as I crossed the finish line. When I heard my race time, I couldn't believe it: 22 minutes, 39 seconds. A personal best! And a silver medal as well, the second-fastest time for my age group, 40-to-49. I'd never been happier to be exactly 40 years old.

On Monday, I came into the office and told everyone about the race and my medal, which I made sure to show them. People were actually impressed with me, something that's never happened before in my life. Emboldened, I bet Golic that he couldn't beat my time, but he refused to accept the challenge—running long distances is boring, he said, and he didn't want to waste his time training for it. In other words, he was scared.

But he did agree to an Olympic-style contest of a handful of events—a real pentathlon, in a way—that would determine once and for all which one of us is the better athlete and better man. Let the Games begin.

PENTATHLON EVENT I: H-O-R-S-E

Date: June 19, 2008
Venue: ESPN basketball court, Bristol, Connecticut

PREGAME INTERVIEWS

GREENY: Golic and I played one-on-one basketball against each other once. We were shooting the opening for our prime-time special in 2004, *Mike and Mike At Night:* a frame-by-frame reenactment of the opening from *The Odd Couple.* There's the part where Felix shoots the basketball and does a little kick with his leg, so we were copying that. Afterward, we decided to play a little one-on-one. Whenever Golic had the ball, he would just stick his butt out and back me down, and there was nothing I could do about it.

But this is H-O-R-S-E, and I'm confident that I'm a better basketball player than he is. I used to be able to clap board back in my day. I can beat him.

GOLIC: "Clap board"?

Official results:
Greeny: H-O-R-S-E
Golic: H-O
Winner: Golic

POSTGAME PRESS CONFERENCE

GOLIC: I used the KISS mentality: Keep It Simple, Stupid. I kept it simple, and stupid lost.

GREENY: What can I say? He found a way to win. He stood there a foot away from the basket and because he's so big, it's not even a real shot for him. He took about 20 of those. Finally, I started missing them. He got in my head.

PENTATHLON EVENT II: TABLE TENNIS

Date: June 23, 2008
Venue: Avon, Connecticut

PREGAME INTERVIEWS
GREENY: We were thinking a racquet sport, and we had already done tennis for our historic "Brawn vs. Scrawn" match, which I won handily. Raquetball? Paddleball? Handball?

GOLIC: There's no racquet in handball, so we settled on Ping-Pong. And about "Brawn vs. Scrawn," I was eating doughnuts between games.

Official results:
Game One: Greeny 21, Golic 5
Game Two: Greeny 21, Golic 12
Winner: Greeny

POSTGAME PRESS CONFERENCE
GREENY: A few days ago, I was in the locker room of my gym and a guy I'd never seen before or since walked up to me, completely naked, and said, "Greeny—Ping-Pong. The key is defense. Just keep hitting it back. Be like a wall."

Even if I was down 20 to 1, I was just going to keep hitting it back—let Golic make a mistake. Eventually, he'd hit it long. Thank you, anonymous naked man.

PENTATHLON EVENT III: RUNNING THE BASES

Date: July 13, 2008
Venue: Yankee Stadium, Bronx, New York

PREGAME INTERVIEW

GREENY: Plain and simple, I want a foot race. Bring it.

GOLIC: At first, this event was going to be a 40-yard dash, but with a 40 you're just running straight ahead. I wanted to add a little something to it, some skill and technique, so we decided on a timed running of the bases—you start in the batter's box and on "Go," you take off. It's not as simple as a sprint. You have to consider where you'll widen out or when to cut a corner. You can slide coming into home plate, or not. This is a thinking man's event.

Official results:
Greeny: 19.29 seconds
Golic: 19.31 seconds
Winner: None. Ruled a tie.

POSTGAME PRESS CONFERENCE

GREENY: I ran first, and let me tell you, when you're standing at home plate, first base looks really far away, closer to 100 yards than 90 feet.

I ran it in 19.29 seconds by The Gnome's watch. Golic came in at 19.33. That's just 0.04 slower. Unbelievably close, and unbelievable—I mean, our high-tech timekeeping was to have The Gnome standing at home, pushing buttons on his Timex. We had a million TV angles of the race including the shot from the blimp, and we did a video review. It came out even closer—I was ahead by just 0.02. So I suggested that we call it a tie. I can't take a win on two-hundredths of a second.

GOLIC: Like the 1966 Notre Dame–Michigan State game and the 2002 All-Star Game in Milwaukee, this will go down as one of the most talked about tie games in sports history.

To be honest, I started running out of gas after I rounded second.

PENTATHLON EVENT IV: MINI-GOLF (MATCH PLAY)

Date: August 4, 2008
Venue: Hidden Valley Mini Golf,
Bristol, Connecticut

PREGAME INTERVIEWS

GREENY: You know what color balls I use? Green. Because I'm Greeny.

GOLIC: The Gnome printed out the rules and regulations of mini-golf earlier this morning. One of them is, "Any conduct that may endanger the welfare of others is prohibited." If I wind up and crush the ball into someone's head and knock them out cold, I'll probably be disqualified.

Official results:
Greeny: Three holes
Golic: Six holes
Winner: Golic

POSTGAME PRESS CONFERENCE

GOLIC: It was a good, fun match. I jumped out to the early lead with a hole-in-one, but then Greeny came storming back late.

GREENY: I'm an avid golfer. Mini-golf? Not as much. I was able to mount a comeback, but then I ran into a problem—my ball was up against the wall. In golf, you usually don't putt with a wall behind you. It hurt my score.

PENTATHLON EVENT V: PENALTY KICKS

Date: August 18, 2008
Venue: Farmington, Connecticut

PREGAME INTERVIEWS

GOLIC: I'm looking forward to this. I'll shoot my five, and then Greeny will shoot his five. If we're still tied, we'll keep shooting until we have a winner.

GREENY: No! I want to do it like the World Cup. They don't go five-and-five. You kick one, then I kick one. One-and-one . . . one-and-one . . . one-and—

GOLIC: Okay, fine, we'll do it your way. It's not worth arguing about.

GREENY: Good. My other question is about protective equipment. Do you think they'll let me expense a cup?

Official results:
Greeny: 2 goals
Golic: 4 goals
Winner: Golic

GREENY: I wanted it so badly. You're the big guy, the athlete, and they liked you. So kids, let this be a lesson to all of you: No matter how much of a loser anyone tells you that you are, if you offer to buy people things, they will like you.

POSTGAME PRESS CONFERENCE

GREENY: I'd like to congratulate Mike on his pentathlon victory and thank all the people who supported me along the way. I want them to know that I tried to do everything I could to win.

GOLIC: Early on, all the kids were cheering for me, but with my second kick, they were booing me. I was wondering what was going on until one of the kids told me that Greeny promised them all ice cream if he won. They were all rooting for Greeny. So I had to ante up as well to get the crowd back on my side.

GOLIC: It was a great move out of you, I have to admit.

FINAL STANDINGS

CONTESTANT	RECORD	GB
GOLIC (USA)	3-1-1	—
GREENY (USA)	1-3-1	2

STINK: I'm saying that there's something inherently wrong with putting a price on injuring people and knocking them out of a game. If you're throwing money into a hat to encourage players to injure one another, that's over the line.

GREENY: Thanks, Stink. So you're wrong, Golic.

GOLIC: Look, bounties are just something that the guys who play defense do. I agree that it sounds bad. Real bad. But does it make you play harder? No. Does it make you play dirty? Of course not. Remember, these players make hundreds of thousands of dollars per game, and they're not going to specifically go after someone for $100, or $500, or a TV. The offense throws a little money around, too. Rashard Mendenhall fumbled the ball a few times during the preseason, so Hines Ward gave him a football and told him to hold on to it all day long; if he put it down or if someone took it away from him, Mendenhall would have to fork over $100.

GREENY: That I get—it's relatively harmless and more in line with the things you make fraternity pledges do. I'd be surprised if the NFL had a problem with that, but the league dispatched two vice presidents to deal with the bounty talk coming out of Baltimore. Clearly they wanted to put an end to it because it's very unappealing.

And what I find equally unappealing are Ray Lewis's comments to Dan Patrick. It's one thing to say "He's done!" in the heat of the moment, but to say it when you know you broke the kid's shoulder and put him out for the season comes across as a taunt. It sounds ugly.

GOLIC: Ray Lewis just told the truth. He was excited about the hit, and he should be. Do you want him to lie? It was a great hit. Every coach in the youth leagues would show that tackle to his kids as a textbook example. As my father taught me growing up, you run through the guy like he's not there; if he doesn't get up, he doesn't get up. You can't worry yourself over it.

GREENY: I think it's important to inject some sanity into this discussion, so I'm turning to our esteemed colleague Buster Olney, a man who knows a lot about baseball and cow-milking. He really wants in on this conversation about football, too. Buster?

BUSTER OLNEY: Isn't this sport one huge bounty hunt? If you're Lawrence Taylor and you wreak havoc on the field and terrorize opposing quarterbacks, you get paid a lot of money. If you're an offensive lineman, you're taught to beat the heck out of the defensive line and steamroll the safeties and cornerbacks. Hurting people is the nature of the sport.

GREENY: But if it's implicit, then why throw money into a hat? It implies that you're now going to try to break someone's knee. You're going to hit someone dirty.

GOLIC: No. You're not trying to hit dirty. Never. And it doesn't change the way you play the game.

GREENY: But if putting a bounty doesn't change the way you play, why is it out there in the first place?

BUSTER OLNEY: I'll bet that when Tiger Woods plays against his close friend Mark O'Meara, they'll put a dinner on it in addition to the prize money. It's that type of thing.

GREENY: Right, but Tiger is trying to sink a 16-foot putt. He isn't trying to land O'Meara in the hospital for a week.

Given that football is a physical sport, I can understand how players can get carried away from time to time, but it's up to the coaches in part to draw the line. Before the season of the bounties, Brian Billick was the head coach of both Suggs and Lewis. What do you think, Coach?

BRIAN BILLICK: Golic summed it up very well. The word "bounty" has a bad connotation to it. As a rule, I believe that no NFL player wants to hurt another player consciously. They're part of the brotherhood, and they realize it could happen to them just as easily.

But with every defense, there's a mind-set of physicality that you're trying to set. The players, they'll huff and puff, but to think that people outside the locker room will understand everything that goes on within a team is either incredibly arrogant or incredibly stupid. At times, I've been guilty of that as much as anyone. When it reaches a certain level, the league absolutely has to address it. Otherwise, it can run out of control very quickly.

GREENY: Thanks, Coach. In fact, the talk of bounties on Hines Ward didn't end with the Steelers-Ravens game. Another division rival, the Cincinnati Bengals, set their sights on Ward as well. There was a lot of bad blood between the two teams, and several Bengals warned that Ward should "keep his head on a swivel" during their next game.

GOLIC: Understand that Hines Ward is the best blocking receiver in the NFL. He will stick on you, and he will hit you. He blocks tough. The first time the Bengals and Steelers met that year, Ward decked Keith Rivers, Cincinnati's first-round draft pick, on a run play. The running back was going outside and Ward, who was running a route downfield, came back and hit Rivers the way every football player dreams of hitting someone. We call it an HBA hit— head hits the ground before your ass. It was a completely clean, legal block. It also broke Keith Rivers's jaw.

GREENY: The Bengals called the hit unnecessary, and a lot of people consider Ward a dirty player. He's a tough guy. I like Hines Ward a lot. But there he was again, playing another week with a target on his back. His response? "They gotta have *their* head on a swivel," he countered. "I always keep my head on a swivel. It's football, you know?"

This is a mentality I need to understand because it's so far removed from anything I encounter in my life. If you know that there's payback coming in your direction, or if there's a bounty on you, what do you do about it?

GOLIC: Nothing. It's probably on your mind, but when you're playing you can't think about it. If anything, it will tick you off even more and make you go after someone. *Get me? Screw that, I'm going*

after you. It's like Sean Connery in *The Untouchables:* You put one of ours in the hospital; we'll put one of yours in the morgue.

The Bengals have every right to be upset over their teammate being knocked out, but don't call it a dirty or unnecessary play. It was Keith Rivers's fault more than anyone else's.

GREENY: Keith Rivers's wired jaw was his own doing?

GOLIC: He started slowing up on the play, and then Hines Ward hit him. You always have to play the game with your head on a swivel to a certain extent—you have to be aware of your surroundings.

As far as the bounty on Hines Ward, he knows that when he catches the ball, they'll try to destroy him. A wide receiver has to expect that in every game. But the play he has to watch out for especially is a turnover, when the defense turns into the offense and can and will go after you. As defensive linemen, we were taught that after an interception, you go destroy the quarterback. You can't do that anymore, though.

GREENY: Do you know what my mentality would be? I would ask out of the game, and I don't think I'm alone. I would not play, period. If players on the other team were saying they'll get me, that I'm going to be carried off the field on a stretcher, I would immediately curl up in a fetal postion. I'm not making this up. I can't handle a confrontation when it's over the phone. People don't even have to be in the same room with me and I get antsy.

I'd tell the coach to just take me out of the game. I'm scared, and I don't want to go out there. The team injury report would have me listed as doubtful because of cowardice. There's a level of toughness in football that, for me, is hard to fathom.

Cris Carter has some strong feelings about what we've been discussing, and he wants in. I yield the floor to CC.

CRIS CARTER: Golic, let me just say that I'm so glad that you and I played on the same team together— but Greeny, am I happy you were never on my team.

Don't worry so much about this bounty talk. It's one of those crazy things about football, and if you don't understand what a crazy sport it is, then you'll never understand the crazy things that go on. Every team that I've ever been on had something. Rewards. I don't want to call it bounties. We had a thing in the locker room where if you drank a gallon of whole milk in one go without throwing up, we'd give you $1,000. Professional football players do a lot of stupid things.

GOLIC: Thanks, Cris. Stuff like that is part of the camaraderie in the locker room, but when you step out on the field, you have to be all business. He's right, it's a crazy sport, and fans want to see collisions and violence. It's what makes football so popular—people go for the train wreck. If there's a bounty out on a player, now they at least know where the train wreck might be.

GREENY: Let me just confirm one thing: In the code among football players, it is accepted to go after another player.

GOLIC: As a rule, absolutely, but you're not going to go after his knees. Clean hits between the whistles. There are lines you simply don't cross.

GREENY: So everyone is trying to knock each other unconscious, and then they all shake hands after?

GOLIC: Right.

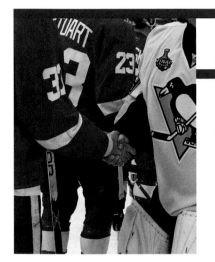

RULE 2.82: Shaking hands after a tough loss doesn't make you any less of a competitor.

GREENY: Not if you ask one of the greatest players in the NBA. After the number-one seed Cleveland Cavaliers were knocked out of the playoffs by the Orlando Magic in the 2009 Eastern Conference championship last year, LeBron James walked off the court without shaking anyone's hand and then refused to attend the postgame press conference.

The next day, James was asked about not shaking Dwight Howard's hand. "I sent him an e-mail congratulating him last night," he explained, "but one thing about me, guys, you've got to understand. It's hard for me to congratulate somebody after you just lose to them, you know? I'm a winner. Somebody beat you up, you're not going to congratulate them on beating you up. I'm a competitor. That's what I do. It doesn't make sense to me to go over and shake someone's hand."

GOLIC: I wouldn't call LeBron an immature brat, even though some of what he said may sound like it. The guy has handled himself incredibly well for just about his entire career, but when you're as big in stature as he is, you just don't do that. You shake hands. It was a mistake.

GREENY: I was surprised. The game was decided an hour before it actually ended; you'd think it would be enough time for the loss to sink in a little. You walk over, congratulate the winner, and get on with your off-season. And as the face of the organization, he should have been at the press conference, too. If you talk after wins, you should talk after the losses, too.

But I can't go crazy on him over this. He's shown himself to be a great player on the court and a good guy, and on the business side he's handled himself ridiculously well. In some ways, he's earned the right to get criticized for this a lot less than other players would. I expect that he'll reflect on it and decide, *You know, I should've shaken his hand,* and move on.

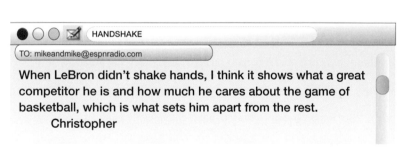

> When LeBron didn't shake hands, I think it shows what a great competitor he is and how much he cares about the game of basketball, which is what sets him apart from the rest.
> Christopher

GOLIC: Get real. Michael Jordan always shook hands after games. I guess you're right, Christopher—basketball just wasn't all that important to Michael Jordan.

GREENY: I remember the last year that Jordan and the Bulls lost to the Pistons, in seven games in 1990—the Scottie Pippen migraine game and the Jordan Rules. Jordan hated those guys, and they hated him. He absolutely was on the court shaking hands after they beat him.

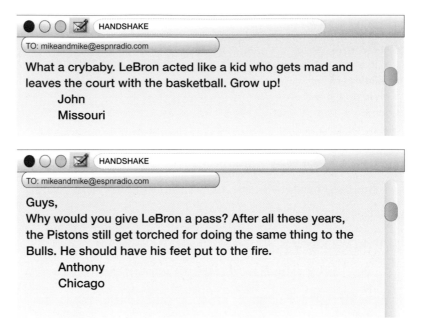

GOLIC: We're not giving him a pass, Anthony, but we're not calling him the worst human being on the planet.

GREENY: And compared to LeBron, what the Pistons did was night and day. For three years in a row, they had knocked Jordan and the Bulls out of the playoffs until 1991, when the Bulls swept them in the Eastern Conference finals. With Game Four out of reach, Isiah Thomas, Bill Laimbeer, and several other Pistons left the bench and walked off the court *with four seconds left on the clock.*

GOLIC: Boy, did they rip the Pistons for that, but fans also got on LeBron, too. It's uglier when there's still time left on the clock. When he was playing for the Vikings, Randy Moss walked off the field with two seconds left in the last regular season game. It was weird—even though the Vikings were losing, they had already clinched a playoff spot—and completely unnecessary.

HANDSHAKE

TO: mikeandmike@espnradio.com

While on one hand I think LeBron should have done the media interview, he has no responsibility to act like he's okay with losing and shaking hands with the other team. We have become a country that hands out trophies for participation. Show me a good loser, and I'll show you a loser.

Michael

GOLIC: Listen, you don't have to go over and slap a high-five and laugh about it. But go over and show some respect for your opponent.

RULE 2.85

No comment? No problem.

GREENY: When you become a professional athlete, you also become a public figure, and you're going to be asked a lot of questions you may be completely unprepared and ill-equipped to answer: Was the league right to suspend a certain player? Is there racism in your sport? How would you react if you learned a teammate was gay?

We're quick to pounce on a player who gives an answer we don't like or want to hear, and we criticize star athletes for not taking stands on the larger issues. Maybe we shouldn't.

Back in the 1990s, I was just starting out as a reporter, and I was assigned to cover the Chicago Bulls on a day-to-day basis. It was immediately after the acquittal of four police officers in the Rodney King beating case, and riots were starting to break out in Los Angeles and other major cities. There was a lot of pressure on Michael Jordan, arguably the most famous person in the world, to make some sort of public statement asking for calm. Jordan wouldn't do it, and a lot of people came down hard on him. But I respected him for it. I felt what he was actually saying was that he didn't know what was going on, and why should he talk about something he didn't know anything about?

No comment? The next time an athlete refuses to answer a question about a topic outside his authority, you should probably stop and think, "Yeah, maybe he's doing the right thing."

GREENY: I'm trying to think back to other situations that I personally witnessed. Here's one: Eddie Belfour, a goaltender in the NHL for many years, was one of the most intense competitors I've ever seen in my life. He was playing for the Blackhawks in 1995 when they lost to the Red Wings in the Western Conference finals in five tough games. The Blackhawks were totally overmatched, but Belfour singlehandedly managed to keep them in every game. He was brilliant, but in double overtime he gave up the winning goal. Belfour skated off the ice and didn't participate in the handshake ceremony that followed. He was criticized by a lot of people for that. But you know, in the moment, with the way it ended, there was a part of me that understood it. You see my point?

GOLIC: No, I don't. There's no excuse for it. None. Belfour's season may have ended quickly—one goal, *boom,* and he was done—but he knew what comes next. He played hockey long enough to know the tradition of sportsmanship that follows.

Look, I've been in some awful losses myself, and I don't think it matters how great a player you are. If you don't shake hands and you excuse it by saying you're a great competitor—no you're not. You're a sore loser.

GREENY: Dick Vitale has been around the game a long time and could probably shed some light on this for us. What do you make of LeBron not shaking Dwight Howard's hand, Dickie V?

DICK VITALE: Well, Mike and Mike, obviously there's frustration. I love seeing a competitor, but that's no excuse. If you can stand tall and face the media when things are going great, then you've got to do it when

ON THE MIKES

By Matthew Barnaby, 15-YEAR NHL RIGHT WINGER AND CURRENT ESPN HOCKEY ANALYST

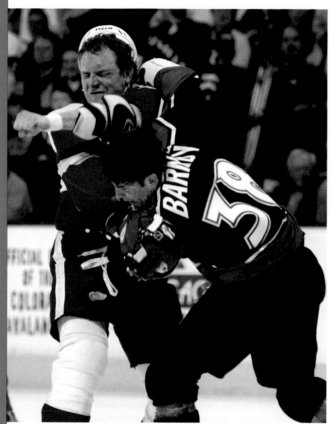

In the NHL, I was known as the guy who got into fights. Lots and lots of fights—some good, and some that were just bad ideas. I made a career out of taking beatings from the likes of Chris Simon, Derek "The Boogeyman" Boogaard, and Stu Grimson, who was known as "The Grim Reaper." This wasn't always the plan. Growing up in Ottawa, I was the top scorer on every team I played for from the age of eight to 14. Once I turned 15, though, I stopped growing, and within a year I was the smallest kid on the ice. When it came time for Juniors, I was drafted last overall, and I realized that the only chance I had of sticking around was to find a new niche. So I decided to fight. I got into 13 fights over the next two days, and I lost every one of them. The coaches must have taken pity on me because they put me in every game that season. And I got to keep playing hockey.

—MIKE AND MIKE IN THE MORNING,
May 14, 2009

RULE 2.87: Sometimes you have to go to Plan B.

they're not. That's just part of the responsibility of being a great athlete.

Obviously, LeBron is a great player, the best I've ever seen at his age. He's awesome. He just hasn't had the help around him that someone like Jordan had. With the Bulls, Jordan had great spacing because teams also had to defend people like Pippen, Cartwright, Paxson, and Kerr. LeBron hasn't had that in Cleveland, and it cuts off angles, et cetera. However, he has to go to the press conference and face the writers and take responsibility for what transpired and for the fact that they didn't live up to what they did in the regular season, where they won 66 games. Sure, they had a tough matchup against a very good Orlando team, but he's got to stand up after the loss. Absolutely.

GREENY: When a game ends, certainly in college basketball, which you coached for many years, the coaches walk across the court and shake hands. What usually happens in those conversations after a tough loss? Is it just, "Good game," or is there more to the conversation?

DICKIE V: It's basically, "Good game." You're down, man. You just got beat. I mean, you congratulate the other guy, but your mind is running wild. What are you gonna say to the media? What are you gonna tell your players? In college, you also have to worry about the moms and dads and the high school coaches, and they're moanin' and groanin' that you recruited their kid and he didn't get enough PT, enough playing time.

Shaking hands with the other coach is part of good sportsmanship. You've gotta get it done. But it's really just a token handshake. I don't care what anyone tells you, it really is.

GOLIC: Thanks, Dickie V. He's exactly right. Unless you know them personally, the handshake is just a handshake. *Nice game.* If they're moving on, *Good luck.* But other than that, you're not saying a whole lot.

You know, you look at golf, and they shake hands after the 18th hole. In tennis, both players always come up to the net and shake hands. They do it in football. They do it in basketball, and they do it in hockey. In soccer, they do it and even exchange jerseys. But there's one sport I can think of where, for some reason, they never shake hands after a postseason series: baseball. They do it in Little League, high school, college, but not in the pros. I'm not saying they're poor sports, but why don't they shake hands?

GREENY: Well, they shake hands with each other, but it's usually in the clubhouse and not on the field of play and in front of anyone. It isn't part of the tradition.

GOLIC: Right, but why not?

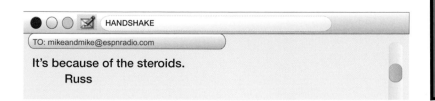

●○○ ✉ HANDSHAKE

TO: mikeandmike@espnradio.com

It's because of the steroids.
　　Russ

WHEN WE COME BACK ON PAGE 92, GOLIC GETS HIS ANSWER, AND LEARNS A NEW WORD.

Just pick a number.

GREENY: The NBA's Ron Artest is an interesting character, and he has a very interesting manner of speaking. Signing with the Los Angeles Lakers, Artest explained how he came to choose his new uniform number:

> "A fan, Trish the Dish, came up with this idea, #37, because I like Michael Jackson so much. RIP Michael Jackson. She said to pick #37 because *Thriller* was the #1 album for 37 straight weeks. It was the greatest #1-selling album of all time, and I feel like I'm #1 in my life."

GOLIC: That's one of the more unique reasons I've ever heard. It was pretty interesting until the last thing he said.

GREENY: I admire Artest for saying it, because the tragedy is that I'm only Number Eight in my life; I'm just not that impressed by me. But to choose your number based on something as comparatively random as the number of weeks *Thriller* was the number-one album on the charts is a little strange. I don't know. I was never a professional athlete. Growing up, I played tennis, but you don't wear numbers in tennis. Every time we've done anything for the show, like throw out the first pitch at a ballpark, we get to wear a uniform, and they ask us to choose a number. I always ask for the number 5, in honor of my father's idol, Joe DiMaggio. But I've always thought that if I was a pro athlete and 5 wasn't available, I would put a lot of time and effort into choosing a number. You come to be so identified with a specific number, and wouldn't it be nice to have some significance with it?

GOLIC: I don't know. I think Artest's reason is a great one, or at least as good as any other. Let's see what our listeners have to say.

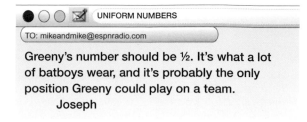

Greeny's number should be ½. It's what a lot of batboys wear, and it's probably the only position Greeny could play on a team.
Joseph

Long thin numbers, like 11, make you look slimmer.
Michael

GREENY: You know, Golic, if you wore 11, you could have been a punter.

I wear 51. I'm a basketball player. The reason? Players on the court is 5, players working as 1.
Chris

Jaromir Jagr wore 68 because it was an important year in his country's history. I always pick 54 because of my favorite movie, *Glory,* with Denzel Washington. It's about the Civil War and the 54th Battalion.
Ben

GREENY: Didn't you give a lot of thought to your number?

GOLIC: None whatsoever. At Notre Dame, they took care of it for me. They gave me my brother Bob's number, 55.

GREENY: See, that's good. Wasn't that nice?

GOLIC: Well, yes and no. Part of me was thinking that he did his thing, and I wanted to do mine, but I had no problem with taking 55. With both my sons playing at Notre Dame now, Jake is a tight end, so he isn't going to get a number in the 50s. Mike, as a lineman, could, but he wanted his own, different number.

GREENY: What was his reason for choosing one number over another?

GOLIC: Well, there was his high school number, 52, but he couldn't get that, either. Basically it's *Okay, what's next?* When I got to the NFL, I was 68 with the Houston Oilers. As a 10th-round draft pick, I wasn't in a position to make a lot of demands. When I went to the Eagles, they gave me 90, and then in Miami I asked for 90, but it was already taken. So they gave me 96.

There was no significance with any of the numbers I wore. When we're throwing out the first pitch at a ballpark now, I ask for 90 because it was the number I played with the most during my NFL career, but there was no reason why I chose 90 in Philadelphia in the first place.

GREENY: I think choosing a number is fascinating, and I would spend so much time on it. I'd drive myself crazy trying to come up with a great number. You know, I almost never play the lottery, but one time I went into a store with a friend and he bought a ticket. I'm thinking that if he buys one when I'm with him and wins $100 million, I'll never be able to live with myself. So I bought one, too. The woman behind the counter asked me what I wanted, and I stood there for 20 minutes, going back and forth choosing my numbers.

GOLIC: Not me. I do random and let the machine spit them out for me. Just pick a number, and you'll be okay.

GREENY: At the end of a postseason series, they usually have a pigpile near the pitcher's mound. They're celebrating like crazy, rolling around on the ground.

GOLIC: Are you kidding me? They go nuts in hockey, too, throw sticks and gloves, and mob the goalie. The other team waits and then lines up to shake hands, so if hockey players can figure it out, why not baseball players? Admit it, you don't know the reason why.

GREENY: Look, I'm the last person on the planet that should be complaining about someone not shaking hands. A handshake is my least favorite social activity. *Hello, it's a pleasure to meet you and, yes, give me some of your germs. Better yet, why don't you cough first?* It's disgustipating. I'll defer to Buster Olney, but I won't shake his hand. Buster?

BUSTER OLNEY: So let me get this straight, Golic. We hear stories of players urinating on each other in the midst of pileups in NFL games, but postgame etiquette is supposedly super-important? Please. The handshakes are all lip service. When baseball players congratulate each other privately after the World Series, that has more meaning than the obligatory handshakes.

GOLIC: Whoa! First of all, I've never heard of players urinating on each other in pileups. I've only heard that players urinate on themselves. Well, one player—Mark Schlereth. But you're not answering the question of why it happens in every other sport except for baseball. Answer me that, Onley!

GREENY: It's *Olney,* you idiot.

BUSTER OLNEY: Okay, I'll withdraw the urination accusation, and I'll make my point this way: During the fight for fumbles, isn't it true that players often grab the manhoods of others in an effort to wrestle the ball away, and after the game congratulate the other team with those very same hands? Baseball players have it right. Let the NFL carry on the charade.

GREENY: Thanks, Buster. But I don't think there's anything *wrong* with shaking hands after. It surely doesn't make you less of a competitor. If anything, it sets a good example.

GOLIC: I've always told my kids or the kids I'm coaching not to look to professional athletes for their role models in life. If you want a role model, look around: Find a relative, or a coach, or a neighbor, a teacher, somebody you can have actual contact with.

GREENY: I think kids can't help but be influenced by athletes, and as a father, it's something I think about with my own children. I'll tell you a quick story. When my son Stevie was three years old, we took a trip together to the toy store. He wanted to get a wooden bat and a baseball, so he picked out a little bat and a little white rubber ball with red stitching on it that looked just like a real baseball. When he handed them to me, I happened to take a closer look at the ball. I noticed that it had Barry Bonds's name on it. My son didn't choose the Barry Bonds ball on purpose; he simply picked it out of a box of 10 other balls that all looked essentially the same. But when I looked at it and saw Bonds's name, I thought, "Do I really want to buy this?" When he wasn't looking, I switched baseballs.

I'm not sure exactly why I did. It wasn't because I was trying to make a huge moral statement. For some reason, I just didn't want to buy him a ball that had Barry Bonds's name on it, especially when there were 10 other balls that were exactly the same except for Bonds's name.

GOLIC: What if it was a Mark McGwire ball?

GREENY: I probably would have done the same thing.

GOLIC: You wouldn't have bought it? What about a Sammy Sosa or a Roger Clemens ball?

GREENY: I think if there was an option, then no, I wouldn't. Again, I wasn't trying to make a stand at the local Toys "R" Us, but given the option of buying a ball that said "Barry Bonds" on it and one that didn't, I chose the non–Barry Bonds ball. When my son's head was turned, I grabbed a different ball from the box, and he never noticed the difference.

After that we went home, leaving behind what had happened at the toy store, and played baseball in the backyard—father, mother, daughter, and son—for the rest of the afternoon. M²M

RULE 2.96: ONE DAY, ATHLETES WILL RULE THE WORLD.

. . . But not yet. How do we know? We asked Liam Chapman, our shaggy-haired producer, to quiz his mum, Shirley Chapman, on some of the biggest, richest, most recognizable athletes in the universe. She's drunk, she's funny, and she's British, and she knows her sports as well as anyone. So we gave Liam's Mum a few pictures and a list of several possible answers for each blank, and we asked her to fill them in for us as best she could. Simple, right?

This is _Tom Brady,_ who plays _football._ He is a _catcher_ for the _Nashville Predators._ Last year, he famously was _elected to the United States Senate from Kentucky._ His fans are known to say, _"Practice? We're talking about practice?"_

This is _Shaquille O'Neal._ She is a _professional golfer._ She won the _World Series_ at the age of 17. Most recently, she won the _Stanley Cup._ She is rumored to be dating _Joe Torre_ and is known for her catchphrase, _"Getcha popcorn ready!"_

This is _Albert Pujols,_ a _goalie_ for the _Indianapolis Colts._ He entered the _LPGA_ at the age of 30. He is known for feuding with _Donovan McNabb_ but quieted many critics by winning the _Heisman Trophy_ last year.

This is _LeBron James,_ who plays _ice hockey_ for the _Minnesota Vikings._ Two years ago, he _threw a no-hitter_ which was unprecedented because _no one did it before._ Then he signed a multiyear contract with the _Minnesota Timberwolves_ and will be _playing center field._ He was in the news last year for scandalously _dating Kim Kardashian._

This is _Steven Gerrard._ He plays _soccer_ for _Liverpool._ His position is _center midfield._ He is the _team captain._ He has won _two FA Cups, two Football League Cups, one UEFA CUP,_ and the _UEFA Champions League._ He is married to _fashion journalist Alex Curran_ and is also _a member of the Order of the British Empire._

This is _Derek Jeter,_ who plays _basketball_ for the _Tennessee Titans._ His nickname is _T.O._ because _people call him that._ Last year, he led his team to the _U.S. Masters,_ which was played in _Cooperstown._ He used to be a _motorcar racer_ but now _wants a new challenge._ People often compare him to the great _Curtis Enis._

RULE 3.49:

Fans Are Crazy Because People Are Crazy.

GOLIC: When my oldest son, Mike, Jr., was red-shirting his freshman year at Notre Dame, he got the chance to travel with the football team to Massachusetts for the big game against Boston College, known as the "Holy War" because it pits the only two Catholic universities with top-tier football programs. I drove up for it, and it was great to see him. I wish I could say the same for the game.

It's not because Notre Dame lost, 17–0, although I'll admit that was disappointing. How or why the Fighting Irish lost, though, I can't say, because I had my own war going on in the stands.

Sitting among the 44,000 in attendance, I missed several key plays, not to mention every kickoff, a blocked punt, a couple of interceptions, and a field goal attempt. I couldn't help it. There was complete chaos in the stands—people were getting up whenever they felt like it, blocking everyone's view, and ordering you to get up from your seat at the worst possible time so that they could get down the aisle.

I was sitting on the very end of a row, and the disruptions were constant. With the **BC** quarterback calling the signals on a key third-and-short play, I heard, *Dude, get up.* You've got to be kidding me. They're about to snap the ball. Get up? After the play, *dude.* They were all completely oblivious to the fact that all the way down there, in the little grassy area, the guys with pads and helmets were trying to play a football game.

At one point, I looked around, stunned by what was going on. Everyone just glared back at me like I was the problem. Then a guy who had gotten up at least eight times already starts walking down the row again. I don't say a word to him. I just give him the death stare.

"Sorry, man," he whimpers, "but I really gotta go to the bathroom."

What am I supposed to do? Tell him to go pee himself?

GREENY: I would've. He has to learn his lesson.

See, you have absolutely no idea what it's like to be a fan. You played football your entire life. I'm always asking you what it's like to be in the huddle, or on the sidelines, or in the locker room. You've been to all those places, and I never have. As a former professional athlete, it's your area of expertise. But in going to the Notre Dame–BC game, you've now entered *my* area of expertise.

Every fan knows that sitting in the stands for a football game stinks. Going to a game is excruciating. It's like a job you hate. It's painful. And let me just say that because you went to a college game, you should appreciate the fact that you missed out on the joy that is blind drunkenness at an NFL stadium.

GOLIC: Oh, I saw some of that, too.

GREENY: But not nearly as much as you would have if you'd been at a pro game. They don't sell beer at college games.

What you have yet to experience—and what a treat this is—is a late-afternoon NFL game. By 4:15, people have been tailgating in the parking lot for four or five hours. They're so blind drunk that their friends literally have to carry them to their seats. Once the game starts, they're on a mission to find someone who's rooting for the other team, pour beer on them, and provoke a fight. It's the only reason they go to the games.

GOLIC: You know, I would lose it. I'd get provoked, for sure.

GREENY: No you wouldn't. No one's going to pick a fight with you. They pick fights with guys who look like me. Are they going to get into it with someone who's 6-foot-5, 300 pounds, and looks like he played defensive tackle for nine years in the NFL? Or are they going to pick on the skinny kid sitting next to him? Trust me—no one's pouring a beer on you.

A quick story about alcohol at sporting events, and an observation: A couple of years ago, I took my daughter, Nikki, who was six at the time, and my eight-year-old nephew, Eric, to a first-round NCAA basketball tournament game. It was at the United Center in Chicago, and we saw Kansas play Niagara. The number-one seed versus the 16th seed—clearly a noncompetitive event, a 25-point lead by halftime. But none of that mattered to my daughter. She was completely into it. Niagara are the Purple Eagles, and Nikki's favorite color is purple, so she's psyched. My nephew is a sports lunatic, and he's loving it. He's staying until the final buzzer. We had great seats, too—right behind the Kansas student section, and the Niagara section wasn't too far away, so we're surrounded by hard-core fans. To be honest, I was a little nervous about this. I mostly go to football games. I've got two young children with me, and I'm expecting that things might get uncomfortable or out of hand. But they never do. Throughout the game, the rival fans are going back and forth with each other in a perfectly friendly, jovial way. Sure, there's cheering and yelling, but no profanities. No fighting, either.

I brought our beloved former producer, Justin Craig, with us, and when we first got to our seats, he offered to go to the concessions stand. Great, I told him, get the kids some popcorn and a couple of beers for us. When he comes back, he's only carrying the tubs of popcorn. "No beer," he tells me. "It's a college game." Now, I can't prove this with absolute certainty, but you don't have to be an Einstein to see the correlation between the exemplary behavior of these die-hard fans and the lack of beer availability at the game.

GOLIC: That's interesting. I thought you were going to say that when Justin told you they weren't selling beer, you ranted and raved and told him not to come back until he got you a beer.

GREENY: In the instant he told me about the beer, I was disappointed. I'll admit it. Having a beer at a game is a time-honored tradition. But in the end, I was glad the evening turned out the way it did.

A beer or two would have been nice, though. For me. But not for anyone else, except maybe Justin.

GOLIC: I understand that people at games want to have a beer or two. Or more. I understand that people drink and have to go to the bathroom. But what I can't understand is their constant interruptions and total lack of awareness. I'm trying to watch a football game but I can't because they're getting in the way. And they could care less.

GREENY: Let me ask you, have you ever been to a Broadway musical?

GOLIC: What are you trying to say? No.

A beer at the ballpark? Absolutely. Nine beers? Well . . .

GREENY: We take the show on the road to Pittsburgh for the opening of the Pirates' new stadium, PNC Park. It's a beautiful spring day, and the place is gleaming.

Everyone's excited, and in the morning we have a contest where people win tickets to come sit with us during the Pirates–Reds game that afternoon.

It's time for the first pitch, and we get to our seats. We're wearing Pirates jerseys that the organization made up for us with our names on the back of them. They're really great shirts, but it also means that we're sitting in the middle of the stands with shirts that say "Golic" and "Greenberg" in huge black letters. In other words, we're very, very easy to notice.

The fans love it, and they start buying beer for us. The entire section—maybe the entire ballpark—is buying us beer, roughly at the rate of one beer per inning. They're sending us beer at the top of the first. By the second inning, we're on our second beer. We don't want to be rude, so we keep accepting, thanking, and drinking. Before the top of the third, another beer magically appears from behind my right shoulder. And on and on and on. . . . Needless to say, by the sixth inning, I'm the drunkest I've ever been in my life.

The radio's staff is at the game, too, but they're upstairs in one of the skyboxes. Meanwhile, Golic and I are sprawled out in the stands, absolutely and completely hammered. The game winds down—the new ballpark doesn't help the Pirates, who drop their home opener, 9–2—and I remember that earlier in the day we said we'd meet up with the staff outside the stadium after the game. I grab Golic.

"C'mon," I tell him. I barely make it to my feet. "We have to go find Willie Stargell's statue."

As a sad coincidence, this was also the day that the great Willie Stargell died, and before the game we decided that it would be a fitting tribute if we all met up at Stargell's statue outside the ballpark afterward.

We stagger down the row toward the aisle when somebody asks us what we're doing.

"We're going to the statue," I say.

"Great! " the voice shouts back. "We're going, too!" About 200 people make their way up the stairs with us and out of the ballpark. We're like the two Pied Pipers of PNC Park. Two very inebriated Pied Pipers.

So me and Golic—and the 200 Pirate fans—go out wandering and, after awhile, I find the statue. We don't see anyone there yet, so we wait. Ten minutes go by. Twenty minutes. Thirty minutes and we're still waiting. Finally, my cell phone rings. It's our producer, Pete Gianesini.

"Where *are* you guys?"

"We're standing in front of the Willie Stargell statute," I tell him.

"Are there flowers and wreaths around?"

"No."

"Greeny, you're in front of the *wrong statue!*"

I look up at the statue for a closer look. Pete was right.

"Damn!" I tell him. "It's *Manny Sanguillen!*"

We leave the Sanguillen statue and keep walking around the outside of the ballpark until we finally see Pete and the crew. Of course, they make fun of me for the rest of the day.

But the embarrassment didn't end there. When we came back to Bristol, I told the story on the air about our misadventure at PNC Park. As soon as I said that I mistook the Sanguillen statue for Stargell's, the show's e-mail inbox is flooded with messages. Every one of them calls me an idiot, and every one informs me that there is no Manny Sanguillen statue outside PNC Park. In fact, there's no statue of him anywhere near Pittsburgh. But there should be, and I could've sworn I saw it.

GREENY: I have, plenty of times. If you get up and leave in the middle of the opera, you can't simply walk back to your seat whenever you feel like it. If you arrive late, you can't walk in until there's an intermission. You can find yourself waiting for an hour or longer. You're not allowed to just walk around randomly and block people's view of *La Bohème* or *Die Fledermaus.* You should start going to the opera.

GOLIC: I don't know about that, but why can't they do the same at football games? If you get up from your seat and leave, you won't be able to go back until there is an actual stop in the action, like a TV timeout.

GREENY: I would be *so* in favor of that, Mike. This could be the Golic Rule in football. When you go to a tennis match, they don't let you get to your seat until there's a side-change—obviously because it's tennis, and you can't distract the players. At many hockey games, the ushers won't let you get to your seat until there's a stop in the action. Why can't they do the same at football stadiums?

GOLIC: It's simple: If you leave your seat, you're going to have to wait in the concourse until the ushers wave you back in, and then you'll have to get to your seat quickly, before play resumes.

GREENY: Let's make sure the Golic Rule is absolutely clear—you're not talking about getting back in between plays. You mean between series.

GOLIC: I'm talking about an actual stoppage, when the music comes on in the stadium and there's nothing happening on the field for a good five, ten minutes. Then—and only then—shall you be allowed to come back to your seat.

The Golic Rule: If you're going to get up and disrupt everybody, stay out.

You like it?

GREENY: I love it.

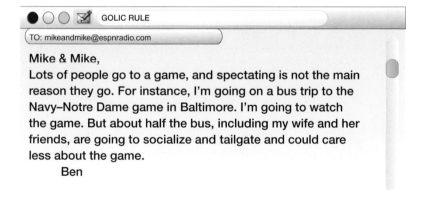

> **GOLIC RULE**
>
> TO: mikeandmike@espnradio.com
>
> Mike & Mike,
> Lots of people go to a game, and spectating is not the main reason they go. For instance, I'm going on a bus trip to the Navy–Notre Dame game in Baltimore. I'm going to watch the game. But about half the bus, including my wife and her friends, are going to socialize and tailgate and could care less about the game.
> Ben

GOLIC: That's fine, Ben. I hope your wife and her friends have a ball. If they want to tailgate, good for them. If they want to socialize by the concession stands, socialize by the concession stands. If they want to socialize with you in the stands, socialize in the stands. Enjoy every minute of it. But don't disrupt my game, and don't be getting up and down during the important parts because you wanna go potty!

> ● ○ ○ ✉ GOLIC RULE
>
> TO: mikeandmike@espnradio.com
>
> Big fan of the show here, and I agree with most of the things you talk about. But please tell Golic that if he wants to watch a game without interruptions, he should watch at home. A lot of people go to games more for the atmosphere. Not everyone needs to sit there and see every play. Thanks.
> Ed

GREENY: Jeez! What is he talking about? We're there to watch a football game. We have paid good money to see this football game, and whatever random thing is catching your interest at the moment is interfering with my ability to enjoy this football game.

This is so disappointing, but I think this e-mail calls for a banning. We may need to ban Ed.

GOLIC: Is he trying to tell me that it's up to him which plays I'll be able to watch and which ones I won't? What should I be watching instead, Ed? If it's halftime and there's a marching band or cheerleaders or something else on the field—okay, I get it. But when the game is being played, what else is there to watch? Is there some other entertainment value I'm not aware of?

GREENY: Ed, we love you, as we love all of those who e-mail us, but in my opinion, you deserve a banning. It's our harshest penalty, one we don't take lightly. In fact, we hate doing it—it hurts us more than it hurts you. But I feel strongly that we need to ban Ed from reading the next 25 pages. Stop reading right now, Ed. Go read something else for 25 pages, and then you can come back and read this book again, but you'll have to pick it back up on page 133. The next 25 pages are off-limits to you. And they're good ones, too.

GOLIC: Wow, that's harsh. Shouldn't we take a vote on this?

GREENY: Fair enough. Let's start with The Gnome. Should we ban Mr. Ed?

THE GNOME: I don't think we should ban Ed.

GREENY: Liam?

LIAM: I'm so-so.

GREENY: Stats?

STATS: He's gone. Put him away for six years.

GOLIC: *Six years?* I think 15 pages might be fair.

GREENY: Okay, we'll compromise and call it 20.

Ed, you've officially been banned from reading *Mike and Mike's Rules* until page 129. We realize the punishment is harsh—God knows what horrible stuff you'll be reading—but we hope you'll use this time to reflect on the error of your ways.

GOLIC: We had to do it, but that was tough.

GREENY: It's never easy, but being a fan means learning the rules, a code of fandom, and I was fortunate to learn them early. I started going to games well before I went to my first day of school. My father would take me, and taught me well. Dad?

WHEN WE COME BACK ON PAGE 114, WE'LL TELL YOU THE ONE THING NO REAL SPORTS FAN WOULD EVER DO.

RULE 3.10: THE BEST BETS ARE NOT ABOUT THE MONEY.

GREENY: In 2002, Golic and I were spending one of the best sports days of the year—the Thursday that starts the NCAA basketball tournament—watching the games together at the ESPN club in DisneyWorld. The place was packed, and 12th-seed Tulsa was giving 5th-seed Marquette a real challenge in a back-and-forth game. With 14 seconds left, Tulsa hit a runner in the lane for the lead, and when Marquette's desperation shot at the buzzer fell short, the underdogs had pulled off a stunning upset. In an instant, half the room was jumping up and down, screaming, "Yes! Yes! Yes!," and the other half was absolutely heartbroken. Golic was one of the ones jumping and screaming, "Yes! I had that one on three of my sheets!"

What?

"I'm playing about 15 sheets," Golic told me.

I couldn't believe it. You can't be celebrating and claiming to have called the upset if you picked the games differently on multiple sheets. You might as well fill in 9.2 quintillion sheets, covering every mathematically possible outcome, and then go around boasting that you had a perfect sheet. Where's the honor in that?

GOLIC: And my thought has always been that I don't care about pride, and I don't care about integrity. I don't even care who's playing, quite honestly. All I want to do is win the pool. I'm in it for the *cay-sh.*

GREENY: For a man who lives in a palace with its own ZIP code to be worried about winning a couple hundred bucks in the NCAA tournament pool is pathetic.

GOLIC: We share our ZIP code with several neighbors.

GREENY: That's beside the point. You should be in to say, "I knew more than all of the others about college basketball." You should have some integrity and play just one sheet. You should play for pride.

GOLIC: And that's the story behind the Sheets of Integrity. We play one sheet against each other with pride on the line, literally—the more ways we can think up to publicly humiliate the other guy, the better.

2004
NCAA DIVISION I MEN'S BASKETBALL CHAMPION:
CONNECTICUT
SHEETS OF INTEGRITY LOSER: GOLIC

GOLIC: Some lady came in, put tape on my eyebrows, and then—OOWWIEE-OWW!!!!—waxed the flesh right off my face. People pay for this? I don't know how you women or Greeny do it.

GREENY: You looked terrific, by the way.

2005
NCAA DIVISION I MEN'S BASKETBALL CHAMPION:
NORTH CAROLINA
SHEETS OF INTEGRITY LOSER: GREENY

GREENY: I had to dress up like the Notre Dame leprechaun for one show. What wasn't part of the bet were the photos, which were later posted online.

GOLIC: You looked terrific, by the way.

2006
NCAA DIVISION I MEN'S BASKETBALL
CHAMPION: FLORIDA
SHEETS OF INTEGRITY LOSER: GREENY

GREENY: Same leprechaun outfit, but this year Golic took it to a whole new level: I had to wear the suit during a live show in South Bend, Indiana. You haven't lived until you've walked the Notre Dame campus at five in the morning wearing a full leprechaun suit, including the boots.

GOLIC: He kept putting his fists up, like you're supposed to, but he didn't look menacing. He looked like he was dancing.

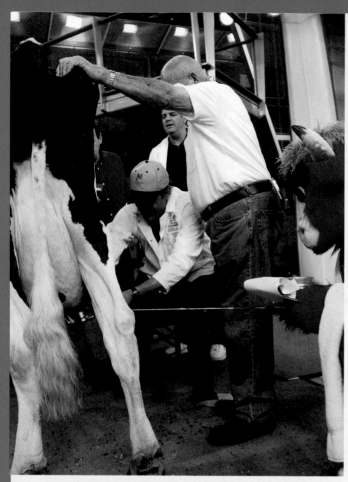

2007
NCAA DIVISION I MEN'S BASKETBALL CHAMPION: FLORIDA
SHEETS OF INTEGRITY LOSER: GREENY

GREENY: I'm a Jewish kid from Manhattan who grew up on Bleecker Street. I've certainly never milked a cow or given it any thought, so Buster Olney, who was raised on an actual farm in Vermont, kindly sent in the rules of cow-milking:

HOW TO MILK A COW
By Buster Olney

RULE NUMBER ONE:
PREPARE THE UDDER.
The cow spent the night lying down in the barn, so there's going to be manure on her udder. Get a hot hand towel, and wipe her down. Then take some Bag Balm and massage her teats. It will help her relax, and she'll allow her milk to come down.

RULE NUMBER TWO:
AVOID PROJECTILE MANURE.
When a cow draws back like she's going to cough, run and hide. If the timing's right, it will come out the other end either at ten miles per hour or at the speed of light. Try to stay out of the way.

RULE NUMBER THREE:
WATCH YOUR BACK.
If you see a cow's eyes get a little bigger and you hear more depth in her moos, don't turn your back to her. If you do, there's a good chance that she'll attempt to mount you. You'll have a half-ton of Holstein over your shoulders.

GREENY: Jeez. I haven't felt that since college, and I didn't enjoy it then.

SOX THE COW: Moo.

GOLIC: The cow had forty pounds of milk in her, but Greeny got only a half-ounce out, if that. He didn't come into work the next day and started complaining about something called "milker's wrist." It was an embarrassment.

2008
NCAA DIVISION I MEN'S BASKETBALL CHAMPION: KANSAS
SHEETS OF INTEGRITY LOSER: GOLIC

GREENY: Four hours before a flight to Louisville, Golic had to compete in an eating contest against three legends of the sport: "Crazy Legs" Conti, "Pretty Boy" Pete Davekos, and Tim "Eater X" Janus. On the menu: wings, wings, and more wings. The winner was Eater X, who ate 31 wings. Golic? A pathetic fourth place in a field of four, with a mere 15 wings.

GOLIC: We had Richard Shea of the International Federation of Competitive Eating in the studio for color commentary, and he was saying things during the contest like, "Golic is a lifelong masticator" and "He'll face the Tina Fey effect—the wings don't look hot, but the more you look at them, the hotter they get." It's not easy to chew when you're laughing.

2009
NCAA DIVISION I MEN'S BASKETBALL CHAMPION: NORTH CAROLINA
SHEETS OF INTEGRITY LOSER: GOLIC

GOLIC: I had to have my legs and forearms waxed. It was very different than the eyebrow waxing, kind of like the difference between a sprint and a marathon. In other words, hours of stinging pain.

GREENY: We had all these long strips of paper lying around with Golic's leg hair on them, so we put one up on eBay. We didn't get a single bid.

ARNOLD GREENBERG: Thanks, Michael. I remember when your mother and I took you to your first basketball game at Madison Square Garden. You were maybe all of two or three years old, and sometimes you'd put your head down. You were a little frightened. The Knicks were playing the Baltimore Bullets. Baltimore had a pretty good player named Jack Marin, who used to really go at it with Bill Bradley. You called him Jack and the Beanstalk. When Marin got the ball, you'd yell, "Jack and the Beanstalk! Jack and the Beanstalk!"

GOLIC: That's the code of fandom?

GREENY: Not really. The rule, Dad?

ARNOLD GREENBERG: Right. The rule is, Never leave a game early. If you go, you might as well see it all. From the time you were little, Michael, you took this rule very seriously. If you went to a game, you weren't going home early. We used to go see the Jets play at Shea in November and December, and it would be freezing. I remember how you'd literally run into the bathroom for a few minutes just to warm up. You were a real trouper, and you always stayed until the end.

Going to a game is like an investment, not of money but time. You've gone through the trouble to get to the stadium; why leave early? Stay and watch the game.

Of course, you stay because you never know what will happen, like the time the Jets were playing Miami on a Monday night several years ago, and they were down by 23 points in the fourth quarter. If you left early, you missed an incredible comeback and the overtime win. Or the year that Namath was hurt in preseason and Al Woodall was the quarterback. They weren't having a good year, but they had a great defense and were leading the Raiders 13–7 with six seconds left in the game when Daryle Lamonica threw a desperation pass into the end zone. Instead of batting the ball down, one of the Jets tried to intercept it, and it bounced off his chest. Warren Wells, a great receiver for Oakland who later went to jail, caught the ball for a touchdown, and the Jets lost. You never know.

Now, there are practical reasons for staying, too. If they're getting slaughtered, everybody at the stadium starts leaving. I always said, let's stay until the end. The traffic out of the parking lot will be lighter, and the longer we sit, the easier it's going to be when we leave. Okay, so they're getting killed. But that's part of the game, and it's part of your memory of the game. Sometimes you play well, and sometimes not.

Watching football with your 5-year-old son is one of the great joys of fatherhood. Until it's not.

 GREENY: When my son, Stevie, turned five, he became obsessed with football. On Sundays, he'd put on his favorite jersey, smear his cheeks with eyeblack, and sit down next to dear old dad for an entire afternoon of watching one football game after another. For me, it was pure joy, one of the best moments in life.

Until the commercials came on.

Commercial breaks during football games have become nothing less than a never-ending barrage of ads for erectile-dysfunction medication. I'm not making light of what can surely be a serious condition, but these ads are constant. The one with the 60-year-old man looking coyly at the 55-year-old woman . . . The older couple sitting in bathtubs and watching the sunset . . . The grinning husband throwing the TV remote out the window . . . The awkward dancing . . . How did this happen? Where did all the Cadillacs and Audis go?

At five, Stevie will ask questions about whatever happens to be on TV. He's asking about everything. So when he turns to me and says, "Daddy, what's this commercial about?" or "Why is that man throwing away his remote?" what am I supposed to tell him?

 GOLIC: Nothing. As soon as the commercial starts, you change the channel. You sit there with the clicker in your hand, ready to switch to something else right away. Just click it.

GREENY: So I don't offer any explanation, just change the channel?

GOLIC: Hopefully you'll find an Alpo commercial and he'll ask about the dog running to his food bowl. Because other than that, you're going to have to lie. If you go anywhere near the truth, he'll ask even more questions, the kind you don't want to answer. Your job as a father is to never let it get to that stage.

GREENY: I already click it whenever a violent commercial comes on, but these ads seem so benign at first.

GOLIC: As soon as you see a 60-year-old guy gardening with his wife and smiling at her, change the channel. Are you ready to answer your five-year-old son's question about why you should call your doctor if you're experiencing an erection that lasts longer than four hours?

GREENY: I'm really not.

GOLIC: Then click the remote right away.

GREENY: I will.

GOLIC: Thanks, Arnold. You know, your dad's rule is a pretty good one.

GREENY: It is if you follow it. I'll explain with another good rule: One of the greatest things a parent can do for his or her children is to take them to their first baseball game.

GOLIC: Oh, yeah. I remember taking Mike and Jake to their first game. It was a long time ago when we were still living in Arizona, and we went to see the Diamondbacks. It's the kind of thing where you save the ticket stubs and put them away in a safe place.

GREENY: Exactly, so when Stevie was four, I took him to his first game. He was already obsessed with baseball, and although he didn't know the names of very many players, he knew Derek Jeter and he knew A-Rod. They were his favorites, and I took him to see a game at Yankee Stadium. It couldn't have started any better. Although we were a little late getting to our seats—by the time we sat down, it was already the bottom of the first—the very first at-bat my son sees in his lifetime is A-Rod hitting a two-run homer. Stevie was ecstatic.

We went in early April, the first weekend of the baseball season, and it was cold, more winter than spring. The Yankees were playing the Orioles, and on the mound that day was Steve Trachsel, otherwise known as the human rain delay. *Oy vey!* He was taking so much time between pitches that I could have gone to the concession stand, bought a hot dog and beer, gotten back to my seat, and everyone would still be waiting for his 3-and-1 slider.

The game was taking forever, and by the fifth inning, the Yankees were down, 7–3. They were getting killed, and I noticed that Stevie was getting a little depressed.

By the middle of the sixth, the wind was swirling around us and we were huddling under our blankets. It was freezing. The Yankees, still down by four and showing no signs of life since A-Rod's first-inning home run, were about to come to bat, and A-Rod was due up. I told Stevie that we can stay and watch one of his favorite players hit, and then we can go home.

"Daddy," my four-year-old son tells me, "let's go home when the game is over."

GOLIC: He did? Good for him!

GREENY: But I'm cold, Mike. Our seats are in the shade, and it feels like the temperature has dropped to seven below zero. They could have held a slalom competition in the outfield, and I can't take Trachsel's pace for much longer. Maybe my son wants to stay, but I'm the adult in this situation. I can outsmart him.

The Yankees go three-up and three-down in the bottom of the sixth. The game drags on until I see my chance during the seventh-inning stretch. "Stephen," I tell him, "the game is over."

GOLIC: In the seventh inning? You lied to your son. It's his first baseball game, and you made him leave?

GREENY: That is correct. He sees everyone get up, but he doesn't know there's more baseball to play—he's four years old. I manage to get him out of his seat and we start heading for the car. I don't mean to suggest that my son is not a genius, but he thinks nothing of the fact that none of the other 50,000 people in the stadium are leaving.

I'm on the highway listening to the game on the radio when Jason Giambi hits a three-run homer in the bottom of the eighth to make it 7–6. There's nothing I can do about it now, and I turn to Stevie in the backseat. "The Yankees are coming back!" I tell him, but I see that his head is straight back and his arms are flailed out to his sides. He's out cold.

Fifteen miles later, it's the bottom of the ninth, and the Yankees are still down by a run with two outs and the bases empty. Thank God, I tell myself, because if they had come back and won this game, I would've never been able to live it down. And then, without warning, the Yankees get a single. Then a walk. Then a hit batsman. The bases are loaded, and coming up to bat is A-Rod. This was the call from my buddy Michael Kay, who was doing the play-by-play for the game:

> The one-two pitch . . . Driven **deep** to center field! . . . Going back is Patterson . . . Still back . . . *See ya!* . . . A game-winning, walk-off, grand slam for Alex Rodriguez! And for one Saturday afternoon here in the Bronx, A-Rod answers the critics with a huge, *hu-u-u-u-u-ge* grand slam to win the game for the Yankees!

GOLIC: You're an idiot.

GREENY: Almost immediately, I receive a text on my BlackBerry from Bob Picozzi.

> tell me ur still at the stadium and saw arods grand slam.

ARNOLD GREENBERG: Let me just add, Michael, that when you were three, we took you to your first game at Yankee Stadium. Your favorite player was Bobby Murcer,

remember? We were sitting in the right field grandstands, and Murcer hit two home runs that day. Both of them landed within 10 rows of where we were sitting, and you were so excited.

GREENY: I feel awful. How does this happen? The one time I break my father's cardinal sports rule—never leave a game early—I rob my son of the first-game experience of a lifetime.

I do have one saving grace, though, which is that my son was fast asleep in the backseat. So I think, "What grand slam?" Now all I have to do is keep Stevie from ever finding out.

The next morning, Stevie wakes up completely ignorant of A-Rod's game-winning heroics. At four, he can't read a newspaper, but just to be absolutely safe I hide the sports section before he can see it. Over the next few days, I enforce a code of silence around him. When Stevie is telling everyone about the game and how he saw A-Rod hit a home run, someone asks us, "Didn't he hit two?" No, I tell him, he did not, and *ixnay* on the *otheray ome-runhay*. As far as my son knows, A-Rod hit only one home run that game, and that's enough.

RULE 3.20: Every true fan should own a lucky couch.

GREENY: Paul Ryan, one of our television producers, brings up what I think is a fascinating psychological question. Without warning, Paul will shave his head completely bald. He says he does this because it's more comfortable, but when he comes in on a random morning suddenly looking like a cue ball, it's very jarring. It's distracting.

Anyway, that's a whole other psychological question. Here's Paul's note:

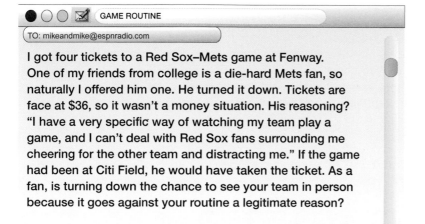

GAME ROUTINE

TO: mikeandmike@espnradio.com

I got four tickets to a Red Sox–Mets game at Fenway. One of my friends from college is a die-hard Mets fan, so naturally I offered him one. He turned it down. Tickets are face at $36, so it wasn't a money situation. His reasoning? "I have a very specific way of watching my team play a game, and I can't deal with Red Sox fans surrounding me cheering for the other team and distracting me." If the game had been at Citi Field, he would have taken the ticket. As a fan, is turning down the chance to see your team in person because it goes against your routine a legitimate reason?

GOLIC: He watches his team in a "very specific way"? Is he kidding? Seriously, dude—take the ticket, sit down, and just watch the game.

GREENY: It's not that simple, Mike. Of course, there are two things at play here. First, Paul's friend has a routine and feels that, for whatever reason, it helps his team, and I believe that to be true. I don't have a specific set of rituals or anything—sitting a certain way, or wearing certain clothes, or a lucky chair—but if I'm watching a Jets game on TV and things are going well for them, I'm not budging. I have to keep watching. For some inexplicable reason, things will change if I leave. It doesn't matter that deep down, I know there really isn't a cause-and-effect to it.

GOLIC: Good. Glad you're finally admitting it.

GREENY: I'm not admitting anything, and I'm not moving, either. Somehow, every time I move, things go wrong. I can't explain it. It just happens.

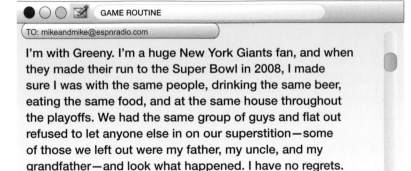

GAME ROUTINE

TO: mikeandmike@espnradio.com

I'm with Greeny. I'm a huge New York Giants fan, and when they made their run to the Super Bowl in 2008, I made sure I was with the same people, drinking the same beer, eating the same food, and at the same house throughout the playoffs. We had the same group of guys and flat out refused to let anyone else in on our superstition—some of those we left out were my father, my uncle, and my grandfather—and look what happened. I have no regrets.

GREENY: See? Three guesses on who beat the Patriots in the Super Bowl that year.

GOLIC: Yep, and this guy's the reason the Giants won. Stop it! I can't believe he excluded his father and grandfather. Think of all the wonderful memories they could have shared.

GREENY: The heck with them. Let me explain something to you. In January 1983, the New York Jets made a run to the AFC championship game, along the way beating the Bengals and the Raiders before they went to Miami and lost the A. J. Duhe game. My family—my father, mother, brother, and me— ate Sunday dinner at the same restaurant every week that month for one reason only: It was working for us, and the Jets kept on winning.

GOLIC: You honestly think a 14-year-old kid eating spaghetti with sausage has anything to do with Lance Mehl intercepting two of Jim Plunkett's passes?

GREENY: It was *working,* Mike. I'm serious. And on some level, I've always blamed the waiter for the loss in Miami. They messed up my order that weekend, but instead of sending it back, I ate it anyway.

GOLIC: You're crazy.

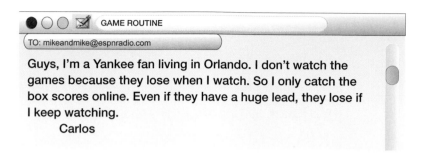

GAME ROUTINE

TO: mikeandmike@espnradio.com

Guys, I'm a Yankee fan living in Orlando. I don't watch the games because they lose when I watch. So I only catch the box scores online. Even if they have a huge lead, they lose if I keep watching.
    Carlos

GOLIC: Wow. According to your definition, isn't Carlos being a true fan? You'll do *whatever* you have to do for your team to win . . .

GREENY: This is a problem. If you're such a fan that you cannot actually watch the games, you've sort of defeated the whole purpose, haven't you? I have one piece of advice for Carlos: Bathe in vinegar. He needs to do something right away to cleanse himself of this spirit.

GOLIC: When I was doing a morning radio show on KGME in Phoenix in the mid-'90s, my partner was Bruce Jacobs, who is a crazy Mets fan. He told me that when he was at Shea one time, the Mets were losing badly. He got up to go to the bathroom, and while he was in the men's room, the Mets rallied. Did he see any of it? No, because he stayed in the bathroom at Shea for the rest of the game. His thinking was that if he went to the bathroom and the Mets started playing better, then he should stay in the bathroom.

GREENY: You can't allow your fandom to go so far that you actually can't watch the game. The whole point isn't reading box scores the next day or hiding in the bathroom, it's seeing your team play and hopefully win.

There's a second thing to consider with Paul's friend, the Mets fan who didn't want to go to Fenway. It's this: The game was at Fenway, and I can completely understand that element of it. The few times I've seen my team on the road in a hostile environment, it was not pleasant.

GOLIC: See, I could understand it if all the guy said was that he didn't want to watch the game with a bunch of Red Sox fans. It's like if you were going to an Eagles game and a friend who's a Cowboys fan wants to join you and wear a Cowboys jersey. Bad idea.

GREENY: I remember when I went to see the Jets at Foxboro for the playoff game a few years ago. I didn't cheer. I hardly said a word, and people were still throwing things at me. I guess they recognized me from the show.

GOLIC: Even if I didn't know you, I'd throw things at you.

●○○ ✉ (AWAY GAMES)

TO: mikeandmike@espnradio.com

C'mon, guys! Don't you know the fastest way to a fan's heart at a game? You buy a couple fans of the other team a free round of beer at the beginning of the game. I promise you that this gesture is enough for them to accept you wearing the away team's jersey and even cheering for them. I buy them a free round, and I always have a great time.

GREENY: I don't know, maybe this guy's a fan of a Canadian Football League team. If you go to an NFL game wearing the visiting team's jersey and offer to buy the hometown fans a beer, it's an explicit invitation for them to pour it on you. They'll drink half of it and throw the rest in your face.

GOLIC: If a guy rooting for the visiting team offered me a free beer, I'd think he probably spit in it, or worse.

● ○ ○ ✉ AWAY GAMES

TO: mikeandmike@espnradio.com

I'm a Dolphins fan, and I live four hours away from Buffalo.
When the Dolphins play up here, I go to the game. We sit
there and get death threats. We have beer and squished
fish thrown at us all game long. We'll keep going, and we'll
wear our Dolphins gear, head to toe.
　　　Doug

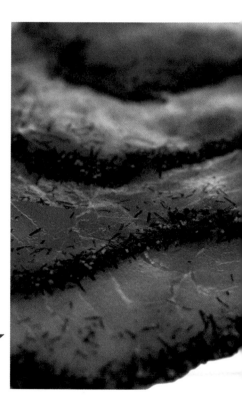

GREENY: They let people bring squished fish into a football stadium? I'm sorry sir, but is that a halibut in your pocket? Gravlax?

GOLIC: Who's Gravlax?

GREENY: It's like smoked salmon, but the fancy way.

● ○ ○ ✉ AWAY GAMES

TO: mikeandmike@espnradio.com

I think the friend needs to go to the game. It's better when
you're a fan of the road team because when you cheer, it
stands out and you feel like you are the team's number-one
fan. Plus, if the guy is single, road fans get more attention
from the ladies.
　　　Cole

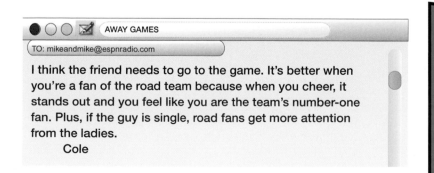

WHEN WE COME BACK ON PAGE 129, GREENY INSTRUCTS GOLIC ON THE PROPER ETIQUETTE FOR VISITING SOMEONE'S HOUSE.

Get it in writing.

When Greeny's Jets were scheduled to play a crucial late-season game against the Patriots on a Thursday night—a game unavailable at Greeny's hotel near Bristol, where he was staying overnight after shooting that evening's *SportsCenter*—he was forced to seek out other places to catch the game. Golic kindly offered for him to come over to his house (where the game could be seen) and, if he wanted, spend the night there. Greeny said he'd think about it. The next day, the Golic family received a fax at their home. ⟶

THE LAW OFFICES OF
GREENBERG & GREENBERG

MIKE GREENBERG
FOUNDER, MANAGING PARTNER, AND NONPRACTICING NONLAWYER

ARNOLD GREENBERG
PARTNER EMERITUS AND FATHER

AGREEMENT made on this 11th day of November 2008 between MICHAEL D. GREENBERG ("GREENY") and MICHAEL L. AND CHRIS GOLIC (the "HOSTS").

WHEREAS, GREENY wishes to have HOSTS provide GREENY with room and board, free of charge, for one evening (the "SLEEPOVER") and, during said evening, be provided with complete and uninterrupted access to the viewing of the NEW YORK JETS versus the NEW ENGLAND PATRIOTS football contest (the "GAME") on a high-definition viewing apparatus with no less than 42 inches of horizontal viewing capability.

NOW, THEREFORE, in consideration of the promises set forth below (all terms specifically accepted by the HOSTS unless they are waived, and any such waiver shall be effective only if initialed by both parties), HOSTS and GREENY agree as follows:

- HOSTS will provide one (1) comfortable and private bedroom and one (1) private bathroom connected to said bedroom for GREENY's sole use.
- Any and all rooms entered by GREENY at any time shall be germ-free and dry. Heating and/ or air conditioning shall be provided to maintain a pleasant and constant temperature.
- No dogs, cats, or children shall be allowed within 15 feet of GREENY's bedroom during the SLEEPOVER.
- Immediately upon his arrival, HOSTS will offer GREENY an unlimited supply of chilled spring water (not distilled), hummus, assorted crudités, and one (1) tray of seedless grapes.
- Periodically, HOSTS will offer GREENY a bucket of extra-crispy fried chicken, which must be served with a clean knife and fork.
- At no time during the SLEEPOVER shall GREENY be required to perform any or all of the following activities: (1) cleaning up; (2) singing; (3) fraternizing with animals; and (4) commenting on furniture, kitchen cabinetry, or family photographs.
- GREENY's bedroom shall have at least four (4) electrical outlets, but no more than eight (8). The bathroom will contain a toilet, sink, shower, four (4) mirrors (one full-length), and will be supplied with toilet paper, fresh bars of soap, newly purchased towels (laundered once for adequate softness), and a clean garbage can.
- Under no circumstances shall any bathrooms have fluorescent lighting and/or nonorganic air fresheners.

Even your most despised rival will have one player you kinda like.

GREENY: In the 1980s, if you lived anywhere outside the New England area, chances are you spent the entire basketball season hating the Boston Celtics. I know I did. I was growing up in New York and was a huge fan of the Knicks. My dad had season tickets, and I didn't miss a single game all year. And I hated the Celtics. Let me be perfectly clear: *hated* them—a strong word, but in the context of sports, it's the only accurate way to describe what fans go through. I hated Kevin McHale. I hated Larry Bird. Parish? Hated him. Danny Ainge? Don't even get me started. But I didn't hate Dennis Johnson.

Though I hated the Celtics with every fiber of my being, Dennis Johnson was the one guy on that team you couldn't help but like. On the court, he was cool. He was classy. DJ was that rare player willing to do whatever it took to help his team win. If it meant taking the big shot, he would take the big shot. If it meant guarding Magic, he'd guard Magic. If it meant making the smart pass, DJ would make the smart pass. Dennis Johnson was simply a winning basketball player, and as a fan of the game, you couldn't help but respect him.

After retiring, Johnson went on to coach in the NBA's D-league. Every year, he was inexplicably passed over for the Hall of Fame. In February 2007, Johnson collapsed after a team practice and was rushed to the hospital. He was having a heart attack, and he died within hours. He was 52 years old. No matter if you rooted for the Celtics, or the Knicks, or the Lakers, or the Pistons, or whoever, if you're a fan, you understood that the game lost something large that day.

GREENY: Where does he get that impression? If it's a hockey game, road fans don't get more attention from the ladies. They get *beaten up* by the ladies.

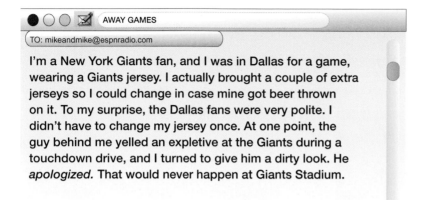

AWAY GAMES

TO: mikeandmike@espnradio.com

I'm a New York Giants fan, and I was in Dallas for a game, wearing a Giants jersey. I actually brought a couple of extra jerseys so I could change in case mine got beer thrown on it. To my surprise, the Dallas fans were very polite. I didn't have to change my jersey once. At one point, the guy behind me yelled an expletive at the Giants during a touchdown drive, and I turned to give him a dirty look. He *apologized.* That would never happen at Giants Stadium.

GOLIC: Amen to that. Either at the Meadowlands or at the Vet when the Giants were playing us, the safest place to be was on the field. We'd be looking up in the stands, and all we saw were the yellow security jackets swarming from one area to another to another.

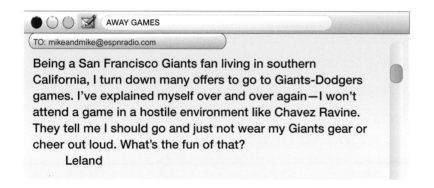

AWAY GAMES

TO: mikeandmike@espnradio.com

Being a San Francisco Giants fan living in southern California, I turn down many offers to go to Giants-Dodgers games. I've explained myself over and over again—I won't attend a game in a hostile environment like Chavez Ravine. They tell me I should go and just not wear my Giants gear or cheer out loud. What's the fun of that?
    Leland

GREENY: From the perspective of survival, sometimes you have to go incognito. In my lifetime as a fan, I try to keep very quiet at road games, and I certainly wouldn't wear anything that identified me as a fan of the visiting team, particularly at a football game. I've even pretended to cheer for the home team just to try to blend in.

GOLIC: So you're going to a game, where normally you would cheer wildly, but since you're going to the other team's place, you won't wear your stuff, and you'll sit there with your hands folded on your lap and do a polite golf clap when your team scores. Are you truly enjoying the game if you can't enjoy the game?

GREENY: I guess it's different for everyone. I'm not a yeller or screamer anyway, but I was at one point. I'd boo like crazy.

GOLIC: The Jets?

GREENY: No. Ivan Lendl.

GOLIC: What's wrong with you? What do you have against Lendl, of all people?

GREENY: *Did.* Not anymore, but I kept after him for years. It didn't matter who he was playing against—say, a first-round match at the U.S. Open against a qualifier—I'd root for the other guy and boo Lendl mercilessly. Then we met at a charity tennis event a few years ago, and he couldn't have been nicer. Lendl and I buried the hatchet, not that he was aware of anything. Our reconciliation took place entirely in my own head, and it was a long time coming.

It started when I was a kid. They would play a tournament at Madison Square Garden every year called the Volvo Masters, and my family would go. The Volvo Masters was a round-robin, meaning that the players on one side of the draw would play each other once, and the top finishers would go on to the semifinals. On the day we went, it was Lendl against Jimmy Connors, so

I was pretty excited. Lendl had already clinched getting through, and if he won the match, he would play Björn Borg; if he lost, he'd go up against Gene Mayer. So Ivan Lendl lost on purpose, and he made no bones about the fact that he wasn't playing hard. He dropped the final set in 17 minutes, and after the match, Connors called him a chicken. But this was the one stinking day that we got the chance to go see the Volvo Masters, and all the fans who had paid good money to go see a player's best effort did not see any such thing. It was the opposite of what my father's hero, Joe DiMaggio, once said when asked why he hustled on a play that didn't have any bearing on the game's outcome. "Because there is always some kid who may be seeing me for the first time," DiMaggio said. "I owe him my best."

So I booed Lendl, and there's absolutely nothing wrong with booing. You're there, you've paid your money, and you should be able to express your feelings. I'm all for it.

GOLIC: Fans do a lot more than that, though. During the 2009 Stanley Cup playoffs, the New York Rangers head coach, John Tortorella, was suspended for one game because he squirted water at the fans in Washington, threw a water bottle over the glass, and then had to be held back by his coaching staff from going after them with a hockey stick. The Rangers filed a protest with the NHL, saying that

there wasn't enough security around the Rangers bench, but the league kept the suspension.

GREENY: You know, the day after it happened, I bumped into Barry Melrose in the hallway at Bristol. Barry used to coach in the NHL and knows hockey as well as anyone, so I asked him if there was any justification for what Tortorella did. Barry Melrose said there was none—Tortorella should have kept his cool in that situation because it happens every single game at every arena; you just have to block it out and not lose your focus. And I thought, "Okay, that makes sense."

But as my day went on, I thought about it a little more. How did we get to a place where it's acceptable behavior to have grown men and women sitting, wearing jerseys, and screaming threats, epithets, curses, and obscenities at people nonstop for three straight hours? There's no other place on the entire planet where you'd say, Oh, that's acceptable. I understand that you have to be a professional and ignore it—I *get* it—but when did we decide that's okay?

GOLIC: The coach has to block it out, and even though it gets tough at times, you have to do it.

Nobody's a robot, though. It's not easy. I know because I had a close call at the Vet one time. Our punt returner had just muffed his second return of the game, and he came off the field and sat down on the bench. I walked over to him, slapped him on the shoulder pads, and tried to offer a few words of encouragement. The fans were really getting on him, one in particular: a guy in the first row, 15 yards from the bench, who was yelling everything you can think to yell at a player.

Athletes you hate mysteriously become more likable as they approach the twilight of their careers.

GREENY: Growing up as a big tennis fan, I didn't like Jimmy Connors at all. If he was playing against Björn Borg, I was rooting for Borg to win. If he was playing John McEnroe, I'd root for McEnroe. Connors versus Guillermo Vilas? I'd root for Vilas. One by one, all those guys retired. Except for Connors, who was still out there, still getting it done, like his incredible run at the U.S. Open. I wasn't expecting it, but I found myself rooting for him like crazy.

There were other athletes. Dan Marino? Absolutely hated him. But then, after many years, I wanted him to make it to the Super Bowl just one more time and finally win a ring. Reggie Miller? Couldn't stand him. I didn't like the flops or any of his other on-court antics. He was always the nemesis of the teams I rooted for, so I rooted against him his entire career. And then . . . all those guys he used to play against were gone, and there was Reggie Miller, still playing. And there I was, rooting for him.

I can't explain it, but if a player I hate stays around long enough, I find myself cheering him on. Maybe it's out of respect. Maybe it's because I've gotten older along with them. Maybe it's something else. Whatever it is, it happens. Does it mean that, if he sticks with it for a couple more years, I'll be rooting for Terrell Owens? It just might.

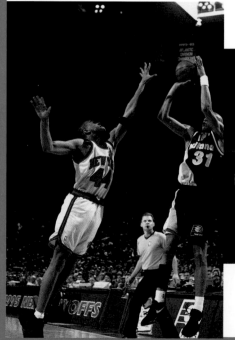

By Tim Legler, FORMER NBA PLAYER AND
CURRENT ESPN NBA ANALYST

It's just assumed that you're not athletic—you're white, after all, so you can't be. I'm not talking about inside the locker room, where your teammates know the kind of athlete you are and what you bring to the team. But everywhere else, it's different. Those who cover the game will refer to you as "a smart player" or someone with "a real blue-collar work ethic," even if it's not true. As a white player, you rarely get the credit you deserve.

A few years ago, I was taping ShootAround in New York City every week, and I'd always stay in the same hotel. I'd check in, and this one guy would carry my bags up to my room. He was young, maybe 20 years old. He was black, and he'd always challenge me to a game of one-on-one. "I've got moves that will break your ankles," he'd say. Or, "Iverson calls me the Answer." I'd give him his tip, thank him, and close the door.

It kept happening every week, and every time I would just tip him and thank him. Then one time, as I was coming down the lobby escalator to go out to get some dinner, the guy was standing at the bottom. "C'mon, one time," I hear. "You'll be crying yourself to sleep." He's trash-talking me the whole way out the door. Maybe I was just tired that day, but I'd had enough and turned around.

"Look, you know where my basketball skills got me?" I said. "I played in college. I played in Europe and the CBA. I played in the NBA for ten years."

He looked at me blankly.

"Where did your basketball skills get you?" I asked him.

After that night, he wasn't asking to play me anymore.

—from MIKE AND MIKE IN THE MORNING,
June 26, 2009

RULE 3.34: It's not always easy being a white basketball player.

I didn't pay much attention to him at first, but he wouldn't stop. I looked up. These were *our* fans? I shouted back a few expletives of my own—basically, I told him to stop talking— but instead of backing down, he started mouthing off at me, too.

I began walking over to the stands, cussing him out the whole way, until one of the cops who was working the sidelines stepped in front of me. He looked me straight in the eye.

"Don't do it," he said. "Just go back to the bench, and we'll take care of it. He's not worth it."

He snapped me right out of it. There's no way I should have even been considering going after that fan, but I'd lost it, and I'm sure glad the cop was there to stop me.

GREENY: Would you have done anything?

GOLIC: Hard to say. It seemed like that's where it was headed. You expect it at away games and not as much in your home stadium. A lot of fans see it as their duty to get on the other team's players and coaches during a game. Before the game, too. We were up in Buffalo at Rich Stadium, warming up in a corner of the end zone about 45 minutes before kickoff. It was still relatively quiet in the stadium, but there were a few guys dressed up in Bills gear right down at the end of the section and within easy shouting distance of us. They were letting us have it, but we weren't paying them any mind. Except for this one guy, who started yelling out for Reggie White.

"Hey, Reggie . . . Reggie . . . Reggieeeeeeee . . ."

He started screaming. "REGGIEEEEE!!! . . . REGGIEEEEE!!!"

I took a look over at him, but I kept on going about my business.

"REGGIEEEEE!!! . . . REGGIEEEEE!!! . . . REGGIEEEEE!!!"

I'm telling you, we were all starting to get distracted. Finally, we told Reggie White just to acknowledge the guy, anything, so that we could get back to our warmups in peace.

"REGGIEEEEE!!! . . ."

Reggie White turned around. "What do you want?" he shouted.

"THERE IS NO GOD!"

And we all started laughing our heads off, except for Reggie—the Minister of Defense, and an Evangelical minister, too—who got very worked up. "You don't say that! There *is* a God! What're you doing talking like that?"

GREENY: I think I'll stick to booing.

RULE 3.36: Everyone's had it with "unknowingly."

GREENY: Because we've gone through a sea change in sports media, fans now have a greater voice than ever before. There was a time, long ago, when sports information was disseminated largely through newspapers. If you wanted to express an opinion, you'd write a letter to the editor, and maybe the paper would run three or four of them on Sunday. In the 1980s and '90s, sports on TV exploded with cable and ESPN, and we saw the rise of sports talk radio, too, the godfathers who created a successful medium from which people like you and me have benefited enormously. And then came the Internet, with its unprecedented access to information and its immediacy. Think about it—if anything happens in the world today and you can't find a video of it on YouTube within 45 seconds, you're screaming at the computer.

Now we have thousands of comments posted online every day as well as hundreds of calls to the local sports talk radio show. Not that everyone's thrilled about it. From time to time, someone—either an athlete or a journalist—will get upset over what's said on the radio or online. I remember how Ken Griffey, Jr., stopped talking to the press after two radio guys in Cincinnati said he shouldn't be playing center field anymore. The way that sports are covered and the way fans relate to athletes has changed dramatically—in some people's opinion, for the worse. But I don't see it that way. I see it as a good thing. No one said you should be taking everything that's said as gospel. It's just one person's opinion, in the same way that what I say is just my opinion.

Now, it just so happens that during this overwhelming surge in information and opinion, we've had to confront the truth about the use of steroids and other illegal performance-enhancing drugs in sports, particularly the extent of steroid use in baseball. It used to be that steroids were brought up only during the Olympics, when everyone thought the East Germans were doing something wrong. Twenty years ago, no one would think of going around accusing this player or that player of juicing. Today, anyone can, and everyone does.

GOLIC: Maybe, but outside of baseball, fans flat out don't care. They surely don't care as much when it comes to football. When someone like Shawne Merriman is busted, the one question most

fans ask is, How soon is he coming back? For the most part, the panic and drama we've seen has been much greater in terms of baseball players.

GREENY: It's not drama, Mike. The problem with illegal steroids? They're *illegal.* I'm not enough of an expert to understand whether they should be legal or not, but they aren't. You can get a doctor to prescribe them for a specific need, but these were people who were illegally taking them and using them in quantities they were clearly not meant for and for purposes they were not meant for. They endangered themselves and—indirectly but in a very real way—endangered the health of thousands of others who felt that they needed to use them in order to have a chance to compete. So what if they weren't being tested for them? At the end of the day, I don't need to be reminded not to break the law. Our boss doesn't come to us and say, "Listen, if you start robbing banks, we're going to suspend you." The fact that it's illegal to inject yourself with something that's meant for racehorses and livestock should have been enough.

GOLIC: You know, I am so tired of all the handwringing over the steroids thing in baseball. How long were amphetamines in the game? Would the players of the 1970s have been able to perform at the level they did, day in and day out, without them? Baseball fans laugh it off, because they don't care about *that.* They laugh about the pitchers who cut baseballs or threw spitters, and nobody talks about putting an asterisk next to strikeouts or voting those players out of the Hall. But steroids? Worst thing to happen in the history of mankind, and anyone who ever touched them deserves to rot.

Listen, taking steroids can be incredibly harmful. Illegal performance-enhancing drugs are bad, bad things. But people act like it's the only thing that ever went wrong in sports and that before the Steroid Era, every player was pure and clean. Wake up, already, because they were not.

GREENY: You used steroids yourself, didn't you?

GOLIC: I did.

GREENY: What happened?

GOLIC: In my third season in the NFL, I dislocated my shoulder during a game. I managed to pop it back in place and get back on the field. Sure, it hurt. It hurt a lot. But with the way I was brought up to play football—if you could walk, you played—I knew that a dislocated shoulder wasn't going to keep me on the sideline. I played with it for the few games that were left in the season, and it kept popping back out in practices and during the games.

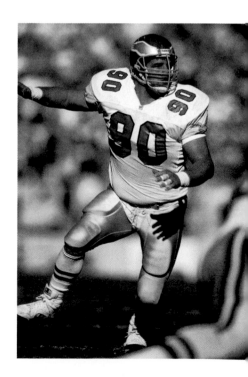

I waited until the off-season to get my shoulder reconstructed. The surgery is called a Bristow repair. They put a pin in there and cut off part of my collarbone. I was in a sling for a few weeks and then rehabbed through the end of February. The Eagles were holding a minicamp in May and I knew that I had to be ready. I'd just come to Philadelphia from Houston, and the coaching staff wasn't very familiar with me. It's not like I was an established star in the league. As a 10th-round pick, I had to earn my keep, and the way to make sure I did that was to be on the field and ready to play. In my head, I knew that I needed to do whatever it took to be on that field.

I did steroids. I took them for the two months before the minicamp, and I did it completely on my own. Not even my brothers knew that I was asking around about them. There was a gym back home in Ohio where my brothers and I used to work out, and some of the bodybuilders there told me that steroids could help me to recover quicker. I didn't tell any of my teammates about it, either, even though taking steroids wouldn't have gotten me in trouble with the league. Of course, it was illegal to have them without a prescription. I didn't have one.

The bodybuilder from the gym in Ohio sent the stuff to me in Philly and explained how a cycle worked. I don't remember if we went over it in person or on the phone. There were injections and pills, and I got enough for six or eight weeks. The first time I injected it, I was scared to death. I didn't know what the hell I was doing, and I didn't know what to expect. I saw effects from it right away and started lifting pretty well, but it got to the point where I didn't like how I was feeling. It throws you out of whack a little, kind of the way you feel when you're starting to come down with the flu. It makes you ornery, too. I remember a guy from Houston who did steroids, and he was a nut case. I didn't beat up people or go out on a rampage or anything, but I probably had a quicker fuse.

At the time, a lot of steroid use was going on in the league. Everyone knew about the Steelers from the '70s. I remember when Steve Courson went public with his steroid use. He was an offensive lineman who played at the same time as me, but it's not like you sit around with other players and talk about what you're

using. They conducted their business, and I conducted mine. You heard things, though, and you kinda knew. But whatever was going on in football at the time, it doesn't justify me using steroids. I did it. It was my choice.

I got better with the injections after awhile, but I never thought it was a breeze. I never looked forward to them. I was nervous every single time.

The steroids worked. By minicamp, I was lifting well and could work out on the field. I got through the cuts, made the team, and got in a few starts that year. I played another six years in the league after that, but I never used steroids again. I was never a strong weightlifter, but there's so much more to the game than strength. There's technique. I could beat guys who were way stronger than me. If you get your hands in the right place, you have the leverage, and it doesn't matter how strong the other guy is. I never thought I needed to be stronger to handle the game.

GREENY: Do you regret doing them?

GOLIC: It's a tough question. They did what I intended them to do. Would I have gone on to play six more years in the NFL if I hadn't done steroids before the minicamp? I'd like to think so, but I don't know for sure. The thing with steroids is, they work. They help you recover quicker and they make you stronger. But steroids alone don't make you a great player.

Do I regret doing them? If you look at where steroids are now, probably. I've told my sons that I did steroids. I also talk to them about not doing steroids. That may sound hypocritical,

I know, but it's how it is. I realize that at some point, Mike, Jr. and Jake will make their own decisions, but I don't want them doing steroids. I really don't. That should tell you something about it.

GREENY: There are different kinds of steroid users in sports, and I think you have to separate them in your mind. There's the majority of them, who were playing pro sports because they were good enough, and they used stuff to get healthy when they got hurt. Like you. Then there are the "roid monsters," guys like Jose Canseco, who acknowledges that he was purely the product of performance-enhancing drugs. Had it not been for the drugs, they wouldn't have been professional athletes. And then there are those who chased records, most notoriously Barry Bonds.

In the court of public opinion, we've convicted Bonds of using steroids, but he was a Hall of Fame–caliber ballplayer before he did them, without a doubt. I don't know if it was his arrogance in believing that he would never get caught, or if it was his overwhelming desire to break the single-season and career home run records and to be considered the greatest player ever to play the game. If Barry Bonds never took steroids, it would be a perfectly legitimate statement to make—he is arguably the greatest baseball player of all time. He would be in the discussion, without question. But now, it's a very different discussion.

GOLIC: But what can you do about it? Are they going to stick an asterisk next to Barry Bonds's records, because if they do that, they should go back to the other eras and do the same for those who they know—they *know*—cheated the game.

GREENY: They wipe out records in track and field, but because it's just you against the field, they can make your performance disappear and figure out how everyone else would have done. Obviously, you can't do that in a team sport.

You know, the day after the Mitchell Report was released, we had Bob Costas on the show. He brought up an excellent point about this. Let's go to the tape:

BOB COSTAS: What baseball should do about the records is a difficult question, and of course people have been drawing their own conclusions. In each case, you don't know to what extent these players used steroids or what effect it had on their performance. In the case of someone like Barry Bonds—and I hate to cite him, because he's not the only guilty party, but he is the most obvious one—the changes in his numbers were so dramatic that they were almost ridiculous. They became video-game numbers, and you can make a direct correlation there. With others, I think the effects would have been more subtle.

All along, I've felt that you can't throw an asterisk behind Barry Bonds's name or Roger Clemens's name because there's just no way to evaluate properly the extent of the advantage. I think the best thing you can do, and maybe the only thing, is to have a page in the front of the record book—and I apologize if you've heard me say this before, but I'll repeat it here— that says something like this: "While baseball has greater historical continuity than any other American team sport, there have always been changes in circumstances as the game has evolved. Those include, but aren't limited to, segregated/integrated; entirely day ball/mostly night ball; pre-expansion/post-expansion; higher mound/lower mound; the advent of relief pitching—and included prominently among these changes in circumstances is the so-called Steroid Era of the 1990s and the turn of the 21st century, and many of the most prominent players in baseball history were involved in that era. Keep all of these facts in mind as you leaf through the pages of this book." And then you turn the page. I think that's the only practical thing you can do.

MIKE AND MIKE IN THE MORNING,
December 2007

GOLIC: Wow. That makes a *lot* of sense. What's more, you now have testing in baseball, with stiffer penalties than in football. If you're caught in football, it's four games for your first offense. In baseball, you're suspended for nearly a third of the season. Without pay, too—Manny Ramirez learned an $8 million lesson.

GREENY: As a fan, Manny felt like the last straw to me. Call me naive, but I truly didn't see it coming. You're going to laugh at me, but I thought Manny Ramirez was as clean as a whistle, a happy-go-lucky guy. And that he was caught taking female fertility drugs particularly bothered me. Is he a slugger, or an octomom?

I can't take it anymore, Mike. I considered myself a hard-line, anti-steroids guy for years, but Manny brought it to a tipping point for me, and I've been beaten into submission. I'm throwing my hands up in surrender. We can't win this fight—I'll still report on it, but I've realized that none of us can stop this thing from happening anymore. Steroids isn't an era—it's here to stay, with no end in sight.

Isn't one of the definitions of insanity to do the same thing over and over again and expect a different result? I can't fight it any longer. We're not winning, and we're not going to win. It's over.

GOLIC: You can't throw your hands up and give up. I'll admit that it's an uphill battle, it's tough, but you have to keep fighting.

GREENY: I'm talking from the perspective of a fan of the game.

GOLIC: Me, too.

RULE **3.45: All's fair in love and football.**

GREENY: In our years of doing the show together, I've started to notice something, Golic. As a lifelong nonfan, you've begun to take on certain characteristics and tendencies of fandom. You didn't really follow sports growing up, did you?

GOLIC: No. I spent my time on the football field or wrestling mat or in the swimming pool. Absolutely, I wasn't a hard-core fan.

GREENY: But I can say with certainty that you're on your way, and I'll tell you why: You've started developing an ever-increasing number of man-crushes. Full-fledged bromances.

GOLIC: I don't know what you're talking about.

GREENY: Mike, you have at least three aspirational bromances. Two are sports-related: Brady Quinn and Michael Phelps. The third is . . . Kenny Chesney. You have crushes on all of them, purely nonromantic crushes, but crushes nonetheless.

GOLIC: Not true. I'm an analyst. I break down athletes' skills or a team's strengths and weaknesses. Brady Quinn and I both went to Notre Dame, and we've become friends. I hope he does well in the NFL, but I break down his ability as a quarterback. When I talk about Michael Phelps, I analyze him as a swimmer.

GREENY: I'm just going to say it: You're in love with Brady Quinn. You are. Every time his name comes up, you get this little smile on your face. When you interviewed him, I saw that look in your eye, and I thought, "You know, those two crazy kids are going to find a way to make it work." You even got his autographed jersey.

GOLIC: It was for my daughter, Sydney.

GREENY: Twenty dollars says that if I went over to your house right now, I wouldn't find Brady Quinn's jersey hanging in Sydney's room. It's in your room, under your pillow.

GOLIC: That's BS.

GREENY: I'm going to have to get confirmation on this from the one person who would know best. Your wife, Chris.

CHRIS GOLIC: Hi, Greeny. I think if Mike was ever going to have a crush on somebody, it would probably be Brady Quinn.

GREENY: Aha!

CHRIS GOLIC: It's a father-daughter thing, I think. It's what they like doing together, a bonding experience. Brady Quinn is good-looking, and he can read defenses. What more could a guy ask for?

GREENY: Thank you, Chris. You're the best.

GOLIC: I can't believe she'd humor you like that.

GREENY: I now have my proof. And what exactly is going on between you and Kenny Chesney? What are you "analyzing" there?

GOLIC: See, here's the deal with Kenny Chesney, and it's not a bro-crush or a man-crush or whatever. We've got a nice little radio show, we get to do a lot of cool things, but I'm not used to running in big-time circles with big-time people. I don't know them, and I certainly don't hang out with them. When we were on Letterman, I got the chance to meet Adam Sandler. We met the president of the United States at the White House, an amazing experience. Kenny Chesney is one of the biggest entertainers out there, so if you want to jump on me for being excited about meeting him, fine. I think it's exciting.

GREENY: It's one thing to be excited; it's another thing to behave like an eighth-grade girl at a Jonas Brothers concert. You know the girls on *The Ed Sullivan Show* when the Beatles first came to America? That's you, my friend.

Now, as ridiculous as it sounds, I'll admit my love affairs, but they've always been about sports. I'll admit to a serious man-crush on Chad Pennington. He burst onto the scene as the Jets' starting quarterback in 2002, and he was tremendous. I kept pointing out how good he was, and I felt you were selling him short. You accused me of liking him a little too much. Fair enough. As a fan, I'm allowed that. If Chad wanted to get together for dinner—have a few beers, a couple of guys hanging out and talking—I'd love that.

GOLIC: I'm calling BS on sports-only crushes, okay? Last I checked, we have a sports talk show. I come into work one day, and what am I doing? I'm not interviewing a baseball player, or a coach, or a reporter. I'm sitting down with a blue Wiggle. Another day, we're not talking about the Phillies or the Chargers or the Cavaliers, we're talking to a Wiggle about Captain Feathersword, the "friendly pirate."

GREENY: Captain Feathersword happens to be a very talented opera singer named Paul Paddick, also known as "the fifth Wiggle." There's Greg, Murray, Jeff, and Anthony, but then Greg had the awful problem with his health and his circulation, so he's not in the band anymore. He's been replaced, which is like the Beatles going on without John Lennon. It just doesn't work.

My kids have since moved on to *Hannah Montana* and *Phineas and Ferb*, but I'll admit that at one time in my life, I was sort of friendly with the Wiggles.

GOLIC: Listen to yourself. *Sort of friendly with the Wiggles.* We lose so much credibility because of you.

GREENY: Maybe, but it's part of being a fan, Mike, in the same way that my love for Chad Pennington is. Or for Leon Washington, although when I said on the air that I wanted to rename one of my children "Leon," I came home to find my daughter, Nikki, giving me a funny look.

For athletes, sports is a game. If you're a professional athlete, it's your job. For fans, though, it's much, much more than that. There are some things about it that make no sense, I'll admit. But then a lot of things don't make sense. Who among us hasn't yelled at a golf ball in flight when we know full well that our screams can't and won't change its direction? And still we yell. It's not meant to be logical. Being a fan is crazy? Maybe. But fans are crazy only because people are crazy. M̲ᴀɴᴅM̲

Behind the Mikes

RULE 3.50: NEVER FORGET WHERE YOU CAME FROM.

GOLIC: In late 1998, my whole family—my wife, Chris, and our three young children—packed up our house in Scottsdale, Arizona, and moved across the country for a radio show at ESPN. My cohost was going to be Tony Bruno. I knew Tony from Philadelphia when he worked for the radio station there. He was one of the originals at ESPN Radio, and a good guy.

So we unpack in Connecticut, my family gets settled in, new schools for the kids, and everything's going great. Tony and I are doing the show, five days a week, four hours a day.

I come in to work one day and there's a note for me from Tony. The note says, *I'm gone.* It wasn't about Tony and me, but apparently some other things had been brewing for a while, and Tony felt it was time to leave. I'm thinking, "Are you kidding me? What's going to happen to the show? Am I going to get canned? I uprooted my entire family for it, and now *this*?"

The suits at ESPN decide to try and seek out other possibilities for hosts. So for the next three months, they fly in various people for auditions, lots of them. There was one guy who did impersonations. He would run out of the studio while we were on the air and call in pretending to be somebody else from a phone down the hall. "Hey there, I'm Joe Paterno!" Or, "Hi Golic, it's Lou Holtz calling . . ." Brutal.

GREENY: I was hired by ESPN in October 1996 as an anchor for ESPN News, and in the summer of 1999 they moved me over to *SportsCenter*. There was a third *SportsCenter* anchor in those days, a comparatively minor role to the other two anchors, but it was still great. I was a *SportsCenter* anchor at ESPN!

A couple of months later, I get a call from the radio department, a guy named Len Weiner. He knew that I had done a bunch of radio in Chicago. "Listen, we've got a little problem," Len says. "We need someone to come in for a couple of days with Golic. Can you do it?"

This was a surprise. "When did we hire Bob Golic?"

"No, no, no," he said. "Not *Bob* Golic. *Mike* Golic. His brother."

I came in very early on Monday, before six in the morning. I had never met this Mike Golic guy before, and I took one look at him and thought, "Wow, what a big, fat *disgusting* slob." He was friendly, but he was also huge and disgusting.

The "On Air" light flashed, and I just felt like making fun of this guy. I'm thinking that if I do it, one of two things will happen. Either he'll laugh and the next two days will be fun, or he'll rear back and punch me in the face. As a Greenberg, I come from a long line of highly litigious people, so if he punches me, I'll sue him for every cent he has. To me, this seemed like a win-win situation.

"You know, Mike, you're a pretty big guy. If the two of us stood next to each other, we'd look like the number 10."

And to his everlasting credit, he laughed.

GOLIC: I had no idea what to expect. I didn't know him. I had never even heard of him, and I couldn't understand how such an incredibly nonathletic, geeky person could ever get a job working at a sports network. And now as soon as we're on the air, he comes on my show and starts *cutting* on me? Huh?

The thing is, it was kinda funny.

My wife listens to the show, and during the auditions she'd call in during the first break, and we'd talk about how it was going. She'd tell me, "Oh, that person's awful," or "This one might have some potential, I can't tell yet," or "Oh, that was *so* brutal." So Greeny's in the chair, and Chris calls.

"Who is that guy who's auditioning today?"

"He's not auditioning. He's just a fill-in. Scheduling problems."

"He sounds kind of geeky, but I think he's the guy."

GREENY: A few weeks later, the ESPN Radio guys call me up. They offer me the job. Completely unexpected. I turned it down. "Thanks, but you've got to be kidding me," I told them. "This show is on so few stations and has a very, *very* small audience. I'm not giving up *SportsCenter* for *that.*"

A couple of days later, I get another call from ESPN Radio. They offer me the job again, but this time they tell me that I'll be able to continue to do *SportsCenter* as well.

So I thought about it. Radio really is a lot of fun, this Golic guy seems okay, and I don't have to give up my spot on *SportsCenter.* This isn't a career move, just a chance to make a few extra bucks. "All right," I tell them. "Let's give it a shot."

But I still thought we'd get canceled. Six months, tops.

RULE 4.01:

The Most Philosophical of All Sports? College Football!

PLATO   ARISTOTLE

Greeny: We've been dissed, Golic.

Golic: Again?

GREENY: *BusinessWeek* magazine recently published a special issue called the "Power 100," where they ranked the 100 most influential people in sports. And there are two things about their list that I'm *really* offended by.

GOLIC: How'd we do?

GREENY: I'll get to that. But first, it's unbelievable to me that anyone could be ranked ahead of George Bodenheimer, the head of ESPN, who in no uncertain terms is a great man and a great leader.

GOLIC: A better man than he is a leader, and he's a great, great leader.

GREENY: And very handsome, too. If the list were accurate at all, George Bodenheimer would be ranked Number One and next would come Number Three—the Number Two slot would be left blank because George Bodenheimer is that far ahead of the rest of the world. Instead, they have him at Number Four. David Stern is Number Three, Roger Goodell is Number Two, and the Number One most influential person in sports is . . .

GOLIC: Liam's Mum!

GREENY: No, it's Tiger Woods. The list was compiled and released before the Woods scandal emerged in late 2009, but even before that, *BusinessWeek* wrote about "how powerful he really is." Now, "power" is a relative word. Tiger was enormously powerful as a draw. He'd earned hundreds of millions of dollars in endorsements and stood to lose hundreds of millions. But this isn't a list of the *richest* people in sports. It's the most influential, and how influential is Tiger Woods, really?

GOLIC: After the scandal broke and the rumors started flying, Tiger announced that he would be leaving the Tour for a while. Someone asked John Daly, who's no stranger to scandal himself, what effect Tiger's decision would have. "Because of

Tiger is why we're playing for so much money," Daly said. "Golf needs Tiger, more than any other player that's ever played golf."

Maybe not Tiger Woods, but there are other people on this list we should be ahead of. It's tough to say how "influential" Number 34 actually is. Don't get me wrong—the guy married a looker, no doubt about it. Nice guy. Great quarterback. But *influential?* I'm referring to Tom Brady.

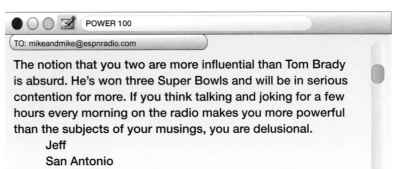

POWER 100

TO: mikeandmike@espnradio.com

The notion that you two are more influential than Tom Brady is absurd. He's won three Super Bowls and will be in serious contention for more. If you think talking and joking for a few hours every morning on the radio makes you more powerful than the subjects of your musings, you are delusional.
Jeff
San Antonio

GOLIC: I'm not ripping on Tom Brady, Jeff; I'm ripping on the list. And what's Tom Brady influencing? He's a great quarterback, but when you see him, what is he influencing you to do? Buy a watch?

GREENY: Tom Brady is usually influencing me to cringe because he's throwing touchdown passes against my team. But I get it with him. He's influential as a crossover star. He's married to Gisele Bündchen, he was dating Bridget Moynahan before, he's talked about on entertainment shows, and he has paparazzi after him. He's one of the few guys in football who gets into all that.

Let's see . . . At Number 50—ahead of us—is the first woman on the list, Danica Patrick.

GOLIC: Number 63 is Don Garber, the commissioner of Major League Soccer.

GREENY: How in the world is Mr. Garber more influential than us? Is America waiting to hear what he has to say about Manny Ramirez or Michael Vick?

We're obviously not doing as well as I thought. I'm a little disappointed. I thought we were doing better.

GOLIC: Wait, at Number 66. Greenberg?

GREENY: Really?

GOLIC: Sorry. It's Ross Greenburg, head of HBO Sports. No relation.

GREENY: And at Number 100, Serena Williams. We didn't make it. It seems that we're not all that influential, and I'm not happy about it. If I had a subscription to *BusinessWeek*, I would cancel it.

GOLIC: To be fair, there are a lot of media executives on the list, but few media people who are in the same line of work as we are.

GREENY: This is a business publication, so of course the list is focused on who is most influential in the finances of sports and not in the actual world of sports. But let me ask you a question, and I think I have an answer: Who is most influential in sports media? It's not us by any means.

GOLIC: I'd think Bob Costas would be high on that list, as would Peter Gammons, but they probably wouldn't be Number One.

GREENY: There are a lot of people who are influential, certainly big talk show hosts like our colleagues Tony and Michael on *PTI.* You'd think announcers would be on the list, but not near the top.

I'll tell you who my Number One might be: the hosts of *College GameDay*—Kirk Herbstreit, Chris Fowler, and Lee Corso. Who has a loud voice in deciding who'll be Number One in the college-football polls, who will play in the championship game, and who will play in what bowl? The sportswriters. Let me tell you something about sportswriters. Their job is to get up in the morning and cover a football game. They go to the stadium, they watch the game, they do their interviews, write their stories and sidebars, and then they go back to their homes or their hotel rooms, and they turn on the television. They hear what Herbstreit or Corso or Fowler have to say, and that goes a long way toward determining who they'll vote for in the polls. And this is not the sportswriters' fault—they can't sit there all day and watch 20 football games.

GOLIC: Whoever is covering Florida-LSU is not going to be watching Texas-Oklahoma.

GREENY: I think the *College GameDay* guys have a *lot* of influence—they influence who will play where in December and January. They actually have an impact in determining the championship of a sport. Peter Gammons may know more about baseball than any other human being walking the planet, but he has absolutely no impact whatsoever on who'll be in the World Series.

GOLIC: And that's the problem with Division I college football. In the pros, the players on the field are the ones who determine who reaches the Super Bowl, and that's the way it should be. If you just took the top team from each conference, the actual winners of the last few Super Bowls wouldn't even have been on the field—the Steelers, the Giants, and the Colts would have been watching the game *from the couch*. Are you kidding me?

Hold a playoff, for crying out loud! Because otherwise you're trying to answer a very tough question: Out of all 120 teams in Division I football, which two should play for the national championship? Part of the BCS rankings is determined by a computer poll, which is actually a combination of six different computer polls. On the human side, there's the Harris Interactive poll, which replaced the AP poll a few years ago. But even though the AP poll isn't included, you can't tell me that a good number of the voters don't look at the AP, so it still surely influences the vote.

Lastly, the BCS also figures in the *USA Today* Coaches' Poll, which has about 60 coaches voting. But let me tell you something about the Coaches' Poll: It's a *joke.* Does anyone really think a Division I coach is sitting around watching 20 or 30 games a week? Most of the time, it's not even the coaches who are voting, it's the sports information director or another school administrator who fills out the ballot. We're left with these polls, and the polls suck.

GREENY: *Playoff, playoff, playoff.* That's all I hear out of you. It's like *Marcia, Marcia, Marcia.*

GOLIC: Everyone wants a playoff in college football, so I could care less what you have to say.

GREENY: You mean "couldn't care less."

GOLIC: Excuse me?

GREENY: You *couldn't* care less. What you just said—"could care less"—actually means you care. If you could care less, then you must already care because you're saying that it's possible for you to care less than the amount of care you already possess. Whereas if you said that you "couldn't care less," then you couldn't possibly care any less than you already do, because you don't care at all. See my point?

The best season is summer.

GREENY: The reason we have football? So that the end of summer doesn't totally destroy you. Like everyone, I love the summer, and without the prospect of looking forward to the start of another football season, Labor Day would be the most crushing holiday of all. Wouldn't you agree?

GOLIC: I like fall the best. I'm a big fall guy.

GREENY: Are you crazy?

GOLIC: I like the weather. Summers can sometimes be too hot.

GREENY: Then why don't you like spring the best? Especially after you've been wearing a coat for months and you notice, Hey, I don't need it today, it's nice again. Only a lunatic wouldn't prefer that.

GOLIC: I like it when it goes from warm to cold, not cold to warm. When it's warm and then all of a sudden it starts getting cool, and you have to put on a long-sleeve shirt, or maybe a sweater, I just love that.

GREENY: You're psychotic. You love fall because of football—your whole life has been football—and I just wish you would acknowledge that.

GOLIC: I like football, sure, but the weather is the main reason I like fall, especially around the time when the hot weather breaks and you need to put just a little something on.

GREENY: But the problem with that time of year is that it lasts for only about ninety minutes, and then it's freezing. You know, we used to have seasons, but not anymore. Now we have Hot, Cold, and Three Nice Days. It's a real shame.

GOLIC: No, because when I say, "I could care less," everyone knows what I'm talking about.

GREENY: But it actually means the exact opposite of what you're intending. It's incorrect, and you say it all the time. Why wouldn't you want to better yourself and say it correctly?

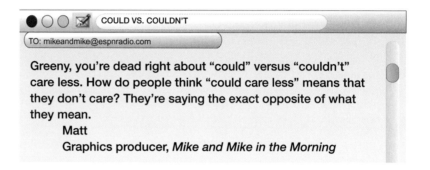

COULD VS. COULDN'T

TO: mikeandmike@espnradio.com

Greeny, you're dead right about "could" versus "couldn't" care less. How do people think "could care less" means that they don't care? They're saying the exact opposite of what they mean.
Matt
Graphics producer, *Mike and Mike in the Morning*

GOLIC: I could care less about what Matt thinks.

GREENY: Obviously, I'm not influencing you at all in this.

RULE 4.62: Bring back the NBA regular season.

GREENY: Everyone is complaining about the BCS system, but playoffs don't magically solve everything, and they can even lead to more problems. Consider the NBA. Growing up, I loved watching NBA games more than anything else. Not anymore. The regular season seems completely optional. What's more, teams have a significant incentive to *lose* as many games as possible. The fewer games a team wins, the more Ping-Pong balls they'll have in the draft lottery, and the greater their chances of getting the number one pick. No one can tell me that the Cleveland Cavaliers didn't tank a season in order to get LeBron James, because that's exactly what they did.

I have a solution that would address both of these issues simultaneously, and I'll humbly refer to it as the Greeny Plan. First, the regular season. The league will never cut the number of regular season games because it would mean losing revenue. I understand that. What's at issue is not quantitative but qualitative.

GOLIC: **That makes no sense, and you're an idiot.**

GREENY: **What I'm suggesting is, don't make the regular season shorter—make it more significant. Cut the number of playoff teams in half, from the top eight in each conference to the top four. Make a postseason berth more of an accomplishment than it currently is.**

Now, you might ask, if only four teams from each conference advance, won't even more teams have nothing to play for by January? Not according to the provisions of the Greeny Plan, which would revolutionize the NBA draft by awarding the top pick not to the lousiest teams but to the ones that won the most games but not enough to make the playoffs. The top pick would go to the ninth-best team in the league, the second pick to the 10th-best team, and so on. Give teams an incentive to win games and play hard every night.

GOLIC: **Would the Greeny Plan keep the lottery?**

GREENY: **Forget the lottery.**

GOLIC: **But how would the worst teams get better? More than any other sport, the NBA draft holds—every year, the best players get drafted with the top five picks, maybe the top 10. It's not like the NFL draft, where you can find a star player in the third or fourth round.**

RULE 4.63

Leave the Ping-Pong balls to Lotto, Bingo Night, and Biba Golic (no relation).

The **NBA** doesn't even have a third round. So what you're saying is that bad teams shouldn't be able to rebuild through the draft.

GREENY: You love to kill all of my ideas, don't you? The Greeny Plan is driving you crazy because you know it's a good plan.

GOLIC: Stop it. All I'm doing is asking questions. You're always getting emotional.

GREENY: I'm not emotional, I'm angry. . . . What was the question again?

GOLIC: How do the worst teams get better?

GREENY: Free agency. Or trades. Or how about *working harder*? Remember, the top overall pick in the draft is not always a great player. Michael Olowokandi didn't exactly turn a franchise around.

GOLIC: Well, let's look at how the Greeny Plan would work in reality. The year that LeBron was drafted, the Trail Blazers and the Lakers were tied with the fifth-best record in the West, and the Hornets had the fifth-best record in the East, but both the Blazers and the Lakers had better records than the Hornets. So it's between those two teams. If we use the **NBA**'s current tiebreaker system, they were 2–2 in head-to-head games, had the same record against division teams, *but* the Lakers had a better conference record than the Blazers by four wins, 33–19 versus 29–23. Under the Greeny Plan, the *Lakers* would have gotten LeBron James?

GREENY: Excellent! And every team would be busting it down the stretch to get that top pick. If you have season tickets to the Knicks or the Bulls, and you're paying ridiculously high ticket prices for your seats, would you rather see your team play with an incentive to win or with an incentive to lose?

GOLIC: No, I agree with that part of your plan. It actually makes sense. But when you talk about teams tanking, let's not include the players as part of the problem. They're not the ones preoccupied with next year's draft pick. It's the organization making situational decisions that puts a team in a losing position.

GREENY: Correct, and there's no better example than the Boston Celtics the year that both Greg Oden and Kevin Durant entered the draft. The storied Celtics, winners of more NBA championships than any other team, were playing 50 years to the day they had won the first of their 17 titles and were honoring several all-time greats who were at the Garden that night: Bill Russell, Tom Heinsohn, Bill Sharman, and Bob Cousy. It was late in the season, and with a record of 23–55, Boston was in position to clinch the second-worst record in the league with a loss against the Milwaukee Bucks. The game was significant not because the Celtics lost. It was the *way* they lost. One of the Celtics players, Ryan Gomes, admitted that his team tanked on purpose to get more Ping-Pong balls in the draft. He *admitted* that teams do it.

Gomes, a terrific college player and a very decent pro, was having a good night in a nip-and-tuck game, scoring 13 points through three quarters. But in the fourth quarter, Gomes didn't score a single point. He couldn't, because he watched the rest of the game from the bench. Asked afterward about his absence, Gomes said, "I probably would have played, but since we were in the hunt for a high draft pick, of course things are different."

AFTER YOU READ WHAT'S ON PAGE 170, YOU WILL NEVER WATCH THE NBA THE SAME WAY AGAIN.

Mike and Mike: Total Access

RULE 4.66: Every king needs a castle.

GREENY: My office at ESPN is on a corner and has two windows. It's big. If I'm not mistaken—and I'm not—it's the nicest office in the whole building. It's phenomenal. I love it.

There's a cubicle near my office. It looks like it's there for an assistant, someone who answers my phone, takes dictation, brings me coffee. The bad news is that I don't have an assistant. The good news? I've got Golic in that cubicle.

That's right. I have an office—an amazing office—and Golic has his tiny cubicle.

A few weeks after I moved in, I asked my kids if they wanted to see Daddy's new office. Of course they said yes. So they came and we went upstairs and down the hall and walked right past Golic slaving away in his little cubicle. And then it was on to my office. They saw how big it is, the windows, the photos of them on my desk and their drawings that I taped up on the walls. Nikki and Stephen took it all in, eyes wide in amazement, and my son asked a question: "Daddy, why do you have an office and Uncle Golic has a cubicle?"

"Because Daddy is much more important than Uncle Golic," I told him.

GOLIC: First of all, my cubicle is not tiny. It has enough room for everything I need—a computer, a phone, a TV, some Twizzlers. Decor? Forget it. Nesting? Don't get me started.

GREENY: It's not about decor or nesting. It's about the one thing that separates an office from a cubicle, and that's the door. The door is vital. I can close the door, and suddenly I'm not in communal space anymore. I'm in my own space. And there's something very comforting about having your own space away from communal space. I can close the door and do whatever I want. I can talk on the phone all day. I can change my clothes. I can even take a nap. I've got my own little wonderful home within a huge office building.

GOLIC: And I'm a man of the people. Most of the folks who work at ESPN have cubicles, and I'm out here with them. We're all together living in our cubicle world. We can see each other as we walk around the place, we can stand up and talk, and I can live with the fact that other people can come over to my cubicle and touch things and I don't have to disinfect everything. I, a man with a cubicle, can visit other people in their cubicles and feel welcomed with open arms.

GREENY: For years I had a cubicle at ESPN. But then one day it hit me: I need an office. I deserve one. I need the space and peace and quiet in order to put up with you as much as I do. So I asked for an office, and I got one. But you didn't, and now you're stuck with your tiny cubicle. Is life fair? Of course not.

GOLIC: But the reason I didn't ask for one—or to be accurate, why I let them give you an office—is because of your psyche. Everyone knows how fragile you are, and I had to give you something so you'll feel more important than me. I'm a giver. Before you moved into your office, you had nothing. You lucked into a marriage—talk about someone outkicking their coverage. You've got two great kids, but at some point soon, they're going to have to take them away from you and teach them how to be athletes because you're certainly not going to do it. You just don't have a lot going for you, Greeny. And if you're in therapy all the time, you won't be able to do the show. I have to give you whatever little bright moments I possibly can, and your office is one of those bright moments.

GREENY: You're right about that: An office is a bright shining moment. And a cubicle is *not*. Everyone dreams of finding work that they love doing, and that's important. Very important. But just as important is having your own office. Earn it. Make it comfortable. Keep it clean and well organized. Treat it like your castle, and treat yourself like a king.

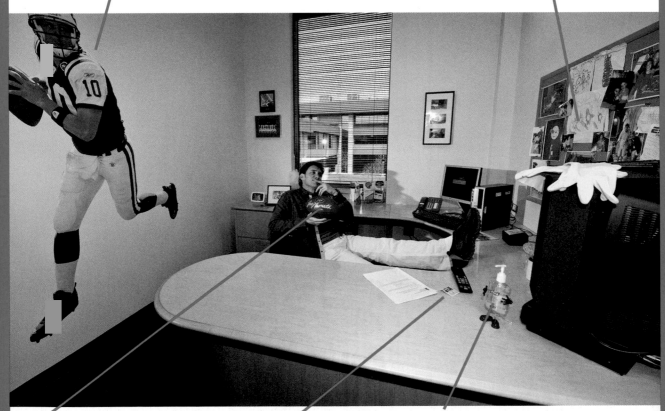

Led Marshall to perfect 13–0 record in senior year and first-ever bowl victory … Rhodes Scholar finalist … Awarded Playboy's Anson Mount Award, which, as everyone knows, honors nation's top student athlete … First-round draft pick, 18th player chosen overall … Brought team playbook on honeymoon … Led Jets to playoffs in first year as starter … Kind of a handsome guy … Yeah, I realize he's with Miami now. Breaking up is hard to do.

"Duck and Chicken Flying over Four Blue Flowers," crayon on paper placemat, 2005, by Nikki Greenberg, age 5.

Signed by the great Joe Namath. A few years ago, he came to Bristol to shoot an interview for ESPN Classic, and there was no way I was going to pass up the chance to meet Broadway Joe. The most excited (and nervous) I've ever been in the presence of an athlete.

Every morning, I have to put up with Golic for four straight hours. My secret? Tylenol, 1,000 milligrams.

Do you realize that the surface of an average office desk contains 400 times more bacterial microbes than a toilet seat? (Don't believe me? Google it yourself.) Not mine, because I make sure someone disinfects it every day. And I never go anywhere without my bottle of Purell. One can never be too careful.

More than 17,000 fans paid good money to see a game that wasn't really a game. I'd have to check the law books, but that sounds like grand larceny to me.

GOLIC: The Celtics wound up getting only the fifth pick in the lottery, not the second, and it served them right not to get Oden or Durant. During the off-season they signed Ray Allen and traded for Kevin Garnett, and they won the championship without the draft pick they were hoping for.

GREENY: But that's exactly my point. You can rebuild without the draft. The Celtics engineered the greatest single-season turnaround in NBA history without the help of a player they drafted.

GOLIC: Okay, changing the way draft picks are awarded under the Greeny Plan is an interesting idea, maybe even a sound one. But if the NBA did that and kept the playoffs with 16 teams, wouldn't there still be an incentive for teams to win?

GREENY: Yes, but those are two separate elements of the Greeny Plan. I'd cut the number of teams making the playoffs because, from the perspective of a fan, if you're playing 82 games and then eliminating only *half* of the teams, the season feels incredibly long and incredibly meaningless. Sub-.500 teams make it in, In the NFL, if an 8–8 team makes it or, say, a 9–7 team wins a weak division while a 10–6 team in a tougher division gets shut out, everyone starts hollering and crying about expanding the number of playoff teams. But that doesn't bother me. It's a good thing when getting into the playoffs is an accomplishment. What does bother me—and it should—is that the NBA

Elect current players into the Hall.

GREENY: There's no reason why you can't. Each sport's Hall of Fame is nothing more than a museum. Do you think the Louvre and the Met had to wait five years after Picasso died before they could hang his stuff?

I've heard the arguments against this, and none are very persuasive. Don't we need the passage of time for a clear-eyed, more accurate perspective? In some cases, maybe, but not for everyone. Was Joe Montana a tough call in 1989? Or Magic Johnson? Why the holdup, exactly?

Would election to the Hall of Fame diminish a player's desire to perform? Of course not. No player worthy of induction would ever let that happen. You think Derek Jeter is going to start coasting because he has a plaque hanging in Cooperstown?

What about the character issue? I'll answer that concern with two words: O.J. Members of any sport's Hall of Fame are no more likely to disgrace themselves in the last years of their careers than they are in the first five years of their retirement, or the first 10 years, or 20. And if someone like Pete Rose had been inducted during his playing career, the Hall would be faced with a choice: either live with it, or throw him out. It's not that complicated.

For some current players (and coaches), induction into the Hall is a stone-cold lead-pipe lock. So what are we waiting for?

Peyton Manning? Hall of Famer. Vote him in, already. Same with Kurt Warner, Tom Brady, Adam Vinatieri, and Randy Moss.

In baseball, is there any doubt that Derek Jeter, Chipper Jones, and Omar Vizquel belong in Cooperstown?

For basketball, Tim Duncan is a slam dunk. Same for Gregg Popovich. And because the sport's Hall of Fame is not just for the NBA, Grant Hill and Christian Laettner should be shoo-ins as well.

And what about the NHL? Martin Brodeur? What's the judgment call there?

Just imagine the marketing perspective that the leagues could exploit and that fans would cherish: *Tonight on Monday Night Football: Three Hall of Famers on the field at the same time!* I'd watch. So would you. So would *everyone*.

Now, please. While we can still buy tickets to see them.

regular season has nowhere near the significance of the NFL regular season. The NBA season feels inconsequential. You could fall asleep for four months and it wouldn't matter.

GOLIC: But if you realize that teams aren't going to stand by and watch 10 or 20 regular season games' worth of revenue disappear, why would they be willing to allow fewer postseason games?

GREENY: The biggest problem with the NBA regular season is that you spend too much time settling too little. I've decided that to play 82 games in order to determine *one* game's worth of home court advantage is not enough.

GOLIC: Home court or home field, I'm not sure if one game makes much difference, either. A lot of coaches prefer to be on the road. It can really focus a team.

When I was with the Eagles, I loved playing in front of the home crowd. Going out onto that field, hearing the fans go nuts . . . I loved it. But there was also something about driving up the Turnpike to the Meadowlands and watching their fans line up to flip us off. You could feel the hate surge inside you. Going into another team's stadium, your team can band together with the feeling that it's not only you against the other team, it's you against all the people in the stands, too, and you think about beating their team and shutting them up.

GREENY: In this era, one game of home court advantage in the NBA doesn't mean nearly as much as it did 20 or 30 years ago. Don't want to throw out the first round and start with four teams from each conference? Fine, but there's going to be major disparity between the top two seeds and the bottom two. The difference between a first seed and an eighth seed can be substantial—15, 20 wins. One game, especially in the first round, is not a sufficient reward. According to the Greeny Plan, we won't give them only one game's worth of home court advantage. We give them *five* home games. If the NBA isn't going to cut down on the number of teams that make it to the postseason, if they're going to keep letting in these measly sub-.500 teams, make the regular season really count for something. Give a 5-to-2 home court advantage to the teams that actually win the games. Better yet, make it a best-of-three series, and let the higher seed host every game.

GOLIC: Good luck getting all the teams to agree to that.

GREENY: Maybe, but the NBA should adopt the key element of the Greeny Plan and get rid of the draft lottery immediately, because for some teams, the lottery has *become* their playoffs. There's no better example of this than a comment made last year by one member of an organization's front office. First, let me preface his quote by saying that I'm assuming he didn't intend for his words to come out exactly the way they did. Sometimes you say something and then you read it in print and realize that it doesn't capture the spirit of what you were trying to say. That said, I don't think I've ever read a quote that looked as bad as this one.

In the spring of 2009, the L.A. Clippers won the lottery and got to pick first overall in the next draft. Almost immediately they announced that they'd select Blake Griffin, the standout power forward from Oklahoma, and within days posted his photo on the team's Web site to advertise ticket sales. Nothing wrong with that at all. But when a reporter asked Neil Olshey, the Clippers' assistant general manager, to tell him when the organization decided on Griffin, Olshey said the following: "I'd say we made the decision in June 2008."

GOLIC: In June of '08? *Before* the start of the season?

GREENY: Correct. Now, I hope he didn't mean to say that the Clippers were planning in advance to be the worst team in the NBA. I'm sure that the front office didn't have a meeting five months before the start of the season and say, "Let's face it, we stink out loud. Always have and always will. We'll stink this year, too, and then we'll get to draft this Blake Griffin guy and completely destroy his NBA career."

GOLIC: You want to give Olshey the benefit of the doubt with his quote, but this is the Los Angeles Clippers, after all.

GREENY: I did want to cut him some slack, but he went on to say more: "When he decided to go back to Oklahoma, we said if we got the number-one pick in '09, he'd be the guy." Does a winning organization think like that? Do football teams sit around minicamp and talk about what they'll do if they finish with the worst record in the league? You *can't* think that way. Why in the world would you think like that? It's as if you're standing over a putt and wondering what the break is going to be on the six-foot comebacker you're going to leave on the green. You can't have a more defeatist attitude than that.

GOLIC: Some people think the glass is half-full. Some think it's half-empty. And then somebody comes along and smashes the glass.

GREENY: Am I making too big a deal out of this?

The Lions should not play on Thanksgiving.

GREENY: It's bad enough having the entire family over at your house on Thanksgiving every year without being forced to put up with the horror that is the Detroit Lions. The Lions have been awful for what seems like forever. My family's flag football team could beat them, and that includes an uncle who always winds up after the meal in the other room sleeping with his pants unbuckled. The final score would be 31–14.

Even the Lions' own fans consider their team to be unwatchable. During their historically futile 0–16 season in 2008, the league blacked out three consecutive home games because of lack of ticket sales. Instead of the Lions, viewers in Detroit were treated to episodes of *Cops* and paid programming. Wouldn't you rather watch infomercials for Ginsu knives and ShamWows, too?

Traditionalists will argue that because the Lions have been playing on Thanksgiving since 1934, the NFL should just allow them to keep playing. But the Lions started playing the holiday game by default because, back then, a game on Thanksgiving was a tough sell. Other cities were reluctant to host it out of concern for low ticket sales, conflicts with local festivities, and lack of municipal services. Are there any pro cities these days that aren't able to host an NFL game because of lack of municipal services? Nope. And yet we're still stuck with the Lions. What's going on here? Are we all living in 1964?

The opposite of tradition is something called *progress.* If we stayed with tradition all the time, we wouldn't move forward on anything. Without progress, we wouldn't have wild-card teams. There would be no *Monday Night Football.* There would be no freakin' *forward pass.*

Still others will cite the devastating financial impact on Detroit if its Thanksgiving game is taken away. Look, I realize that the state of Michigan has undergone some awful economic turmoil in recent years, and the people who are suffering there have my utmost empathy. But the economic future of Detroit never has and never will revolve around a single game. In baseball, the Cincinnati Reds used to play host to the first game of the season every year— "opening the Openers"—but now there's a season opener the Sunday night before. Last time I checked, the city of Cincinnati is still standing, is it not?

We've had enough. No more Lions football on Thanksgiving.

Can we please get the Steelers?

GOLIC: You're not. It's a loser's mentality. The Clippers seem to be in the lottery almost every year, and maybe they've gotten used to it. It seems as if they see no way of climbing out of the hole, and it's just seeped into the core of everybody there. You sure don't hear Bill Belichick saying stuff like that.

GREENY: That's a good point. You didn't hear Belichick saying that when Sam Bradford announced that he'd be staying for his senior year at Oklahoma, he pulled Bob Kraft aside and told him that the Patriots should pick him in case they lost more games than anyone else. You don't hear even the Lions saying that, and they went 0–16. But the Clippers clearly aren't thinking about the playoffs. Their hope is watching Ping-Pong balls shoot out of a hopper. They really do stink on ice.

It's a shame. Blake Griffin is a fun, highly marketable player, and I hope he doesn't fade away. But I wonder, are the Clippers the worst organization in professional sports?

GOLIC: The Raiders are bad, but they got to the Super Bowl not that long ago.

GREENY: The Lions?

GOLIC: They had their 0–16 season, but they're still not as bad as the Clippers. In baseball, you have the Royals and definitely the Pirates, who set the record for most consecutive losing seasons.

GREENY: I'm going to have to recuse myself from talking about losers because, in some ways, I'm a born loser myself. I'm 42 years old, and all my life I've come up small in big moments.

GOLIC: Yes, you have. I can attest to that.

GREENY: Particularly in anything that requires a certain degree of athleticism. I've never been the greatest athlete in the world. No one would ever confuse me with Jim Thorpe. Anytime I've had to do anything of significance athletically, I've shriveled. And it's the same for me outside of sports. The first time we were on Letterman, I could barely speak, and you wound up doing all of the talking. In big spots, I'm not good.

GOLIC: The first time I saw you play golf when people were actually watching you, you were an embarrassment.

GREENY: I was, but things have strangely begun to turn for me. I don't understand why, but I know the exact time and place where it happened: on the pitcher's mound at Wrigley Field, June 26, 2008, 6:54 P.M.

GOLIC: When we threw out the first pitch? I was sure you were going to find a way to back out of it and save yourself the embarrassment. The week before, you were running around the office telling everyone that you were going to shake off the first few signals from the catcher. For a *ceremonial pitch*? You would've gotten both of us banned. So finally you dropped that idea and came up with a different scheme, the surgical procedure excuse.

WHEN WE COME BACK ON PAGE 180, THE MOST EMBARRASSING MOMENT OF GOLIC'S CAREER.

When in doubt, ask your mother.

Does Mike Mussina (270–153, 3.68 ERA, 2,813 Ks) belong in Cooperstown? We asked Peter Gammons, who said yes. We asked Buster Olney, and he said yes, too. Tim Kurkjian said yes. Bob Picozzi, who isn't officially a voter but holds opinions we highly value, said no. We say no, too. But there's another person's opinion we absolutely needed to hear: Liam's Mum. She's the mother of our shaggy-haired producer. She's drunk, she's funny, and she's British, so we asked Liam to get her thoughts on the matter. An actual conversation between one man and his mother:

LIAM: Hi, Mum. How are you?

MUM: Good, Liam. And how are you?

LIAM: Good. I need your help on a straw poll we're doing. Is Mike Mussina a Hall of Famer?

MUM: (pause) . . . Yes.

LIAM: Why is that?

MUM: Because he's good at what he does.

LIAM: What sport does he play?

MUM: Football.

LIAM: Nope.

MUM: Basketball?

LIAM: No.

MUM: Motor racing?

LIAM: No. Not motor racing.

MUM: Ice hockey?

LIAM: No.

MUM: Then it's basketball.

LIAM: No. It's not basketball.

MUM: I give up.

LIAM: Mike Mussina plays baseball.

MUM: Didn't I say that?

LIAM: No.

MUM: Oh.

LIAM: How do you think he compares to Bert Blyleven, John Smoltz, Curt Schilling, and Tom Glavine?

MUM: I think he's a little better.

LIAM: What would you say is Mussina's biggest strength?

MUM: His persistence to win.

LIAM: Very good. And, Mum, at the end of the day, what will he be remembered for?

MUM: For giving it his best shot.

LIAM: Great. Thanks, Mum. Take care.

MUM: Okay. Love you.

GREENY: It deserves mention that, on the day before I was scheduled to pitch, I was in a surgery room in the hospital with an injury that would have landed any ballplayer on the 15-day DL.

GOLIC: Mention it? You were scripting a four-part miniseries. Did you have Tommy John surgery?

GREENY: Almost. I had a small, benign cyst drained from under my arm.

GOLIC: Big deal. It's like my father's rule: If you can walk, you can play. Loosen up your arm and throw the ball. It's one stinking pitch!

That's the one thing I've learned about you—the drama that you create out of thin air.

GREENY: All the pressure was on me that day, Mike, not you. If you got up there and threw the most feeble pitch in the history of the game, we all would have had a good laugh over it because you played in the NFL for nine years. No one can say that you didn't have a certain level of athletic ability and skill. Me? I'm the little skinny guy. The loser. If I screwed up the pitch, I would've been written off for good. *Poor Greeny, but what did you expect? He did the best he could do. . . .*

I'll admit I did not throw a major league pitch that night. I simply tossed the ball to the guy standing 60 feet, 6 inches away, and he tossed it back to me. Before a packed ballpark, I got the job done. It was one of the great athletic achievements of my life.

GOLIC: I'm just happy we didn't get booed.

GREENY: Oh, *we* didn't get booed. *You* did. You short-hopped the pitch and got way booed.

GOLIC: I probably deserved to be booed, but so what? I was going to fire one in there. An honest fastball. Someone from the Cubs' front office pulled me aside before the pitch and offered me his advice. "Aim your throw a couple of feet higher than the catcher's mitt," he said. "Trust me." Of course I didn't listen to him. I spotted the catcher, started my windup, reared back, and threw heat.

The problem was, I was stepping off the mound as I released the ball, so the pitch went straight down. Since when did they raise the pitcher's mound?

GREENY: About 150 years ago, give or take.

GOLIC: The Wrigley pitch honestly screwed me up a little. A year later, we got an invitation to throw out the first pitch at the Jake in Cleveland. My hometown. I was stressing the whole flight out there. Once we got to the ballpark, it started to rain, so I just sat there during the delay, thinking.

GREENY: I didn't notice. I was walking with a swagger all day. I was completely confident, the new me.

You know, I kept the ball from Wrigley, and I'm never giving it up. Growing up, I was a huge baseball fan, but I thought the closest I'd get to a pitcher's mound at a major league ballpark was a good seat three rows behind

the dugout. You played in some of the greatest stadiums in the country (and also the Vet). But for me to walk up there in front of a packed house was one of the most memorable experiences during my years at ESPN.

There's something about Wrigley that makes it a very special place. I lived in Chicago for 11 years, and if you include all the games I covered as part of my job, I've been there at least 200 times. I should be used to it by now. But every time I walk though the gate, every time I see the infield, the ivy, the brick walls, the bleachers, the scoreboard, it gets to me. There's something about Wrigley that's different from any other ballpark.

GOLIC: For me, it's having one of those Italian beef sandwiches that they sell there, a very special experience.

RULE 4.82: There are seven great cathedrals of sports in the United States. You should definitely visit them all.

GOLIC: There's Wrigley and Fenway Park, Lambeau Field, Churchill Downs, the Indianapolis Motor Speedway, and two others that we'll let everyone argue about.

GREENY: No, just one. Because another is definitely Augusta National. I went over to my sister-in-law's one year to watch the final round of the Masters, and it's almost amusing to hear the reverence with which the announcers talk about Augusta. She commented on it, and I started thinking that you either buy into it completely or you mock it. I buy in. I love it. I'm completely into Augusta.

GOLIC: Of all the majors, I like watching the British Open the most because the conditions really humanize the players for me. I get a kick out of watching them struggle. But if I could win one of them, I'd love to win the Masters, for sure. I buy into it, too.

GREENY: The time at the in-laws was the year Kenny Perry held the lead by two strokes with two holes left to play. On the 17th green, he blew a chip shot for par, and right after that, he bogeyed on 18. It was heartbreaking. Perry had the Masters in his sights and could almost feel the green jacket around his shoulders, yet he couldn't close it out. To be fair, standing over a golf ball when you need to make a shot is the most difficult thing to do in all of sports. Ted Williams famously said that hitting a round ball with a round bat is the hardest, but I think the golf shot is harder. I'm sure people who've never played golf or who have played very little would laugh at that statement—the golf ball isn't moving, and there's no one impeding you. It's not like you're trying to throw a football 30 yards on a dime as a 290-pound lineman is getting ready to put a helmet in your ribs. Or the purely physical act of trying to turn on a 100-mile-an-hour fastball—that sounds harder, too. But I don't think it is. I think trying to hit the big golf shot is the greatest challenge of all.

GOLIC: Here's the thing about a golf shot: time. In football, there's the 40-second clock, so you know that, no matter what, you're going to have to run a play within that amount of time. In baseball, if the pitcher is winding up, you'd better be ready to hit that pitch. But in golf, you can look the shot over, you can address the ball, you can step back, the wind might start blowing, you can step back again, take one more look at it, change clubs . . . It can mess with your head. And even with the top players, it can mess with their heads.

GREENY: How those guys have that level of mental toughness, I have no idea.

GOLIC: But I disagree, because I think Ted Williams was right. The hardest thing is hitting a baseball. Take Joe Carter—coming up to bat in the bottom of the ninth, two outs, runners on, you're down by a run, you're facing a pitcher you're batting 0-for-4 against, the crowd's going nuts, and you have to block all of that out and just make something happen. There's the physical challenge and the mental challenge, and then there are your teammates, too. There are a lot of people you're swinging the bat for.

TOUGHEST SPORT

TO: mikeandmike@espnradio.com

You're nuts, Golic. I'll put you over a 12-foot putt for a million dollars, and you'll be shaking so bad that the putter will fall out of your hands. In golf, you never hit the same shot twice. I'll give you six months of learning how to hit a 100-mile-an-hour fastball or six years of learning how to play golf. You'll be able to hit the baseball, but you'll still stink at golf.
    Chris
    Minnesota

GOLIC: Baseball's not just about learning how to hit a 100-mile-an-hour fastball. What if it's a sinker, or a slider, or a curve that's coming right for your head but then drops over the plate? It's not just about sticking a bat out on a pitch you know is coming.

GREENY: When you're in the batter's box, you don't have as much time to think. The pitcher's going to throw the ball at any second. When he does, you've got to be ready to react. In golf, you're walking, you're waiting, you're hanging around, and it's entirely up to you to decide when you're going to start the play. And on some level, it's easier to react to what someone else does. In baseball or football or basketball, what you're doing out there, in part, is seeing what the other guy is doing and reacting to it. There's none of that in golf.

GOLIC: But you know exactly what you have in golf. You know it's a 12-foot putt that breaks a little bit right to left. In baseball, you have no idea what's coming.

GREENY: Let me tell you, if you knew exactly what you had in the 12-foot putt, you'd be the greatest golfer in the world.

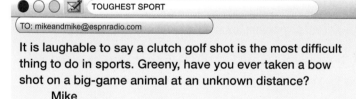

> **TOUGHEST SPORT**
>
> TO: mikeandmike@espnradio.com
>
> It is laughable to say a clutch golf shot is the most difficult thing to do in sports. Greeny, have you ever taken a bow shot on a big-game animal at an unknown distance?
> Mike
> Pensacola

GREENY: As a matter of fact, the last time I took down an antelope with a bow and arrow, I did find the pressure to be somewhat excruciating. The time alone in your own head when you're up on the antelope stand . . . Look, I've said this many times before: My people do not hunt.

GOLIC: And it's one thing to stalk an antelope with a bow and arrow. If you want pressure, try taking down a grizzly that's charging you.

GREENY: Maybe not antelopes, but we got an e-mail later from a listener named Jorge that brought up a great situation: penalty kick in the World Cup. Pressure of self, pressure of team, pressure of nation. Your entire country is living and dying by that penalty kick, literally in some cases. Horrible things have happened because fans lose all sense of perspective.

GOLIC: The goalie is just hoping to get lucky because the kicker has such a ridiculous advantage. And you're right, they're nuts to a level that we in this country can't understand. Some of the things that happen after the loss of a soccer game—people losing their lives—blow my mind.

GREENY: Even taking the horror of that out of the equation, it must be an enormous amount of pressure to know that your entire nation is depending on you. I remember when it happened in the finals of the 1994 World Cup, which was held in the United States. I covered a couple of the games, but I wasn't there for the final in the Rose Bowl between Italy and Brazil. I was watching it on television, and it went to penalty kicks. Roberto Baggio from Italy was up, one of the best players in the world, the reigning FIFA player of the year, the guy who scored two goals to get his team into the final. And he missed it. He kicked it over the crossbar, and Brazil won the World Cup. That missed penalty kick is now part of Baggio's legacy. He's the Italian Scott Norwood for the rest of his life.

GOLIC: What about this: A big free throw in the **NBA Finals** to tie the game with no time left on the clock. Not a free throw to win, because if the game is already tied and you miss, you'll just go to overtime. It's only you and the ball, 15 feet from the hoop. You might have hit this shot a million times in practice already, but you've never been in this kind of situation before.

GREENY: But I think golf skews the debate. People have a harder time giving the credit that's due in that situation. It's easy to pooh-pooh golf because the level of athleticism is relatively nonexistent when you compare it to the level that's required to play professional football or basketball. Baseball isn't the most athletic sport, either, but certainly it requires a set of physical tools in order to play the game well. Golf, in many ways, requires none of that. If as a kid I worked as hard as I could every single day, I still wouldn't be a football player. No matter how hard I tried, I just wouldn't become big enough, strong enough, or fast enough. But despite my limited physical attributes, I still

could have become—theoretically speaking, at least—a professional golfer. That's not the point. The point is that I'll never be able to hit a 100-mile-an-hour fastball. Throw a touchdown pass in the Super Bowl? It will never happen. And I have no better chance of ever making that 20-foot putt to win the Masters, either.

GOLIC: A lot of athletes are physically gifted, but not everyone is a superstar. When you talk about the greatest in history, all of them have athletic ability, no question about it. But they also have unbelievable minds. The battle that you're waging against yourself and the mental aspect of that challenge is often the difference between reaching your goal and falling short. I talk about this all the time with my kids.

GREENY: Right, and when it's just you and your shot, is there a more daunting adversary than yourself? The older I get, the more I believe that to be true, not only in sports, but in anything. You can have all the talent in the world and all the skill in the world, but the only thing that separates you from success or failure is your own mind. The battle is magnified in golf in a way that it isn't in any other sport.

Sometimes, the hardest thing to do is to create complete silence in your own head. It's like when you wake up in the middle of the night and you have a lot going on in your life. You start thinking about things. Your mind starts to whirl. Pretty soon, you're thinking about everything. Well, that's what you're fighting against when you're setting up to hit the golf shot. You can't stand there and think, "If I make this shot, a shot that's at a distance I've tried maybe 25,000 times before in my life, a shot that could win me the Masters, the most prestigious golf event in the entire world, a shot that my family will celebrate forever, a shot that will define my career" . . . you can't let any of those thoughts enter your head. Your mind has to be silent.

It's hard to understand the level of mental stamina required of pro golfers, and it's why one of my favorite events in sports every year is the "Can You Break 100?" challenge, run by *Golf Digest* magazine, the USGA, and NBC. Days before the U.S. Open, a foursome of three celebrities and a contest winner—a regular guy—go out and try to break 100 on the tournament course. In the first year, the celebrities were Tony Romo (who shot an 84), Justin Timberlake (98), and Matt Lauer (100). John Atkinson, a 39-year-old sales manager from Omaha and father of three who was diagnosed a year before the contest with inoperable lung cancer despite never having smoked, won the contest and shot the round with them. An inspiring story, Atkinson shot 114 in front of the glare of the cameras.

GOLIC: It was great to see Atkinson play the round at Torrey Pines, just a great story.

GREENY: Do you know who was the first celebrity to sign up for the following year's challenge? None other than Michael Jordan.

GOLIC: He's a really good golfer, too. Lemme ask you, do you think you could break 100?

GREENY: Under those conditions? I would have *zero* chance. I probably wouldn't even come close. Jordan is about a one handicap, and I'm a 16. I don't think it comes as a surprise to anyone that Michael Jordan is a better athlete than me, and a much better golfer.

WHEN WE COME BACK ON PAGE 196, WE'LL BE JOINED BY PAUL SIMON AND WILLIAM SHAKESPEARE.

A Tale of Two Staffers

What's it like working on the *Mike and Mike in the Morning* show? Well, it can be the best of times and the worst of times. Here's the way **The Gnome** (producer Scott Shapiro) and JOAQUIN (associate producer Curt Kaplan) saw the same period of July 12–16, 2008. Apparently, and for some reason, Joaquin is not allowed to leave the state of Connecticut.

July 12

The Gnome: It's Saturday night and I'm at a concert in Central Park, the heart of New York City, for the start of the 2008 All-Star Game festivities. I arrived in the city earlier in the day to start work for the week's shows, but now it's time for a little fun and relaxation. Just as the concert is about to start, I'm presented with the opportunity to move up from deep within the 60,000+ in attendance to the very first row. No, I didn't score a lucky ticket. I'm here with a group of us from ESPN, including Michael Kay, the Yankees' play-by-play announcer and 1050 ESPN radio host. The security guys recognize him, and before I know what's happening, we're getting waved up until we're right in front of the stage. Luck by association! And what a show it was. Headlining the concert was none other than Jon Bon Jovi, who electrified the crowd nonstop for more than two hours with hits like "Livin' on a Prayer." No complaints here.

JOAQUIN: It's Saturday night, and the Slurpee machine at my local 7-Eleven is down again. When the red light's on, it means that the Slurpee is still "cooking," and if you try to get one, it comes out too watery. So I wait. Fifteen minutes later, I give up. I get myself a hot dog instead. I hang out in the parking lot until I'm sleepy.

July 13

The Gnome: It's early Sunday afternoon, and I'm at Yankee Stadium for the All-Star Legends and Celebrity Softball Game. Talk about celebs—Billy Crystal, Spike Lee, Whoopi Goldberg, Chris Rock, and George Lopez, to name a few. And a Who's Who of Hall of Famers, too, including Ernie Banks, Ozzie Smith, George Brett, Wade Boggs, Dave Winfield, Paul Molitor, Gary Carter, Tony Perez, Goose Gossage, and Rollie Fingers. Thanks to Mike and Mike's involvement as event announcers, I get to ride their coattails and spend the game in one of the Yankee Stadium dugouts. Simply being in the place where Mickey Mantle, Lou Gehrig, and Joe DiMaggio once roamed provides me with plenty of joy on its own, but to be surrounded by all of the Hall of Famers and celebrities is more than a wide-eyed 28-year-old could ever ask for. Everyone's quite pleasant and polite, and I can sense that many of the celebs are in awe of the surroundings, too.

JOAQUIN: Sunday, late afternoon. Someone knocked on my apartment door. (That's right, I have an apartment. Greeny says I live in a refrigerator box under a bridge in Hartford, but that's a joke. It's not funny.) Anyway, I heard someone knock about an hour ago, but I can't figure out if they're still there or not. I have to be very quiet. It's starting to get dark and I want to turn the lights on, but that would be a bad idea.

The Gnome: Early Monday morning, and it's time for my day job, the actual *Mike and Mike* shows! And what better place to be than historic Grand Central Station, where we shoot all four hours amid hundreds of thousands of commuters during the morning rush. Talk about a big-city vibe, and great exposure, too. We're fortunate enough to have David Ortiz and Bud Selig as guests, as well.

After the show, I get a couple more hours of work in, take a quick nap, and then meet Golic for a subway ride back up to the Bronx for the Home Run Derby. I've been to derbies in the past, but I was especially looking forward to this one because it would be one of the last signature events at the old Yankee Stadium. I spend a half-hour on the field, right behind the batting cage, watching the All-Stars take their practice swings.

I should have left after batting practice because of the 3:30 A.M. wake-up call for the next day's show, but I decide to stay for the entire first round. I want to see everyone bat once. And wow, am I glad I stayed! It was a rather ho-hum evening at the ballpark until the final hitter, Josh Hamilton, dug in. Hamilton's story is tremendously inspiring, and tonight he put on an electrifying display of one colossal home run after another. It was like seeing a Hollywood story come to life before my eyes. As he belted 28 home runs in Round One, all I could do was stand in amazement. One more incredible moment for a ballpark that has seen so many.

JOAQUIN: Monday afternoon. Dr. Phil can be a real hardass sometimes, but this guest totally deserves it—he has issues with his daughters' boyfriends. To me, his anger is an outward expression of his hurt, fear, and frustration. But what a jerk. Way to go, Dr. Phil. You tell him. I'd write more, but *Life After People* is about to start on the History Channel. Gotta go.

The Gnome: Another show from Grand Central, and Greeny's parents, who live in New York City, stop by to say hello. Greeny introduces me to them. "You call him 'The Gnome'?" Mrs. Greenberg asks her son. "That's terrible. You can't call him that." All I can say is that a mother is never wrong. After the show, Greeny's parents take the Mikes and me out for real-deal pastrami sandwiches at Mendy's. What a treat!

JOAQUIN: In the morning, I ██████████████████████████

████████████████████████████████████

████████████████████████████████████

██████████████████████████████ (I've been advised by counsel not to discuss any actions that occurred or may have occurred on Tuesday, July 15, 2008.)

The Gnome: It's Wednesday morning, and we've all returned to our usual digs in Bristol, Connecticut. You'd think that being back at the home office after four days of nonstop thrills would be a letdown. Not so fast. Because today Mike and Mike have the honor of launching ESPN Radio's fourth annual Don't Give Up ESPYs V Foundation Auction. There are so many great experiences to auction off throughout the show, including our premier item—a four-hour *Mike and Mike* live broadcast from the highest bidder's home. We're thrilled that two bids were offered at $57,100 each and, in order to raise the most funds possible, we decide to accept both and broadcast the show twice from the road. By the end of the day, ESPN Radio's V

Foundation Auction raises a cumulative total of more than $1.13 million. For me to play a part in such a meaningful cause is truly humbling.

JOAQUIN: I love the V Auction. Three times during the show, we play parts of Valvano's speech from the 1993 ESPYs. If I was allowed to work only one day per year—I've had actual dreams about this—today would be that day.

I get back home around 3:00 P.M. Later, I think I hear somebody getting beat up outside my window. Can't say for sure.

Later that same day

The Gnome: Because of the tight schedule, we have no choice but to rush to the airport immediately after the show. Next on the itinerary: a flight to the nation's capital for my first-ever visit to the White House.

The reason for our trip is President George W. Bush's annual T-ball game on the South Lawn, with Mike and Mike serving as honorary public address announcers. Participating in the T-ball games is one lucky child from each of the 50 states and the District of Columbia. In the president's words, the event is an opportunity for "players and fans to come together and celebrate this wonderful game." And what a celebration! Mike and Mike start off the festivities by introducing President Bush, the first lady, Honorary T-Ball Commissioner Frank Robinson, and Kenny Chesney, who sings the national anthem. After the first game, Mike and Mike welcome the president, Robinson, and Chesney back onto the field with U.S. Postmaster General Jack Potter, and together they unveil a new stamp commemorating the 100th anniversary of "Take Me Out to the Ball Game." Chesney then leads us all in the singing of the ballpark classic.

One major thrill for me is my seat location. I'm two rows in front of President Bush and the first lady, and one row in front of Kenny Chesney. And somehow I wind up sitting right next to the U.S. ambassador to Japan, J. Thomas Schieffer.

After the T-ball, I'm part of a small group walking with the president, the first lady, Greeny, and Golic from the field to the White House. The president informs us that he loves the show. Could you ask for a higher compliment? The fact that the most powerful man in the world enjoys the product that I pour countless hours into every day is an exceptional feeling.

Later that day, the president hosts a reception in the Rose Garden celebrating the sport of baseball. It was a perfect, picturesque evening with the sight of the Washington Monument emerging from beyond the White House gates and the Rose Garden flowers appearing as a virtual work of art. Kenny Chesney gets up and gives a surprise outdoor performance, delighting the crowd with six songs. I honestly have to pinch myself. Who am I to deserve the opportunity to sit in the Rose Garden of the White House for a private performance from a *Billboard* superstar? Then the president takes the mike and says, "It doesn't get much better than this—country music in the Rose Garden and celebrating baseball." Yes!

Afterward, a small group of us are escorted into the West Wing of the White House for a private tour. And wow, is this tour special! We spend 20 minutes in the Oval Office learning about every nook and cranny—the significance of the rug, the blinds, the portraits. We take notice that the president's desk is remarkably clean.

We leave the White House grounds late, well after 10:00 P.M., and head back to the hotel. I still have to get some work in for the next day's show. Our location will be the Newseum here in D.C., with a view of the Capitol in the background, and the guests will include George Will and Senator and Hall of Famer Jim Bunning. With any luck, I'll be able to squeeze in a few hours of sleep tonight. I'm emotionally spent. The days flew by so fast, and it was worth every second of time that I poured into it. It was certainly a week to remember.

JOAQUIN: I stop by the office, but no one's around. I make some crank calls.

GOLIC: To apply for the contest, people were asked to submit a six-word essay. Can you believe it? That's my kind of essay. Where was that homework assignment when I was in school?

GREENY: It's much harder to write a good six-word essay than it is to write a good 600-word essay.

GOLIC: Are you kidding me? I'll take my chances with the six-word essay.

GREENY: Well, that's just you.

GOLIC: No, it's most of America. If you gave someone the choice between writing a six-word essay and a 600-word essay, we all know which one they'd do: six words. End of story.

GREENY: It depends. What are you trying to accomplish with it? To write something that's six words long and worth reading is harder.

GOLIC: *Everyone* would pick the six-word essay.

GREENY: So what you're saying is that everyone would choose to do the harder thing?

GOLIC: No, that's not what I'm saying, because I don't agree that it's harder.

GREENY: If you think it would take you longer to write a good 600-word essay than a good six-word essay, you're wrong. It's very easy to come up with a six-word essay that gets you dinner. *Honey, I would like the steak.* But it could take you an entire lifetime to write a good six-word essay.

GOLIC: Or 20 seconds. It's amazing how wrong you can be. When we opened this up to our listeners and asked for their submissions—the winning prize, an autographed photo of Liam and Joaquin—how many did we get?

GREENY: Okay, we got 5,350 entries in less than an hour, 32,100 words of essay, but that doesn't mean that all of them were good essays, or even most of them.

GOLIC: They weren't bad:

> Greeny is out of his mind.

> You, my friend, are an idiot.

> Can I buy you a beer?

> I need to line my birdcage.

> I gotta dog. Named him Mike.

I like that last one a lot, but maybe you want to rewrite it in 600 words because you think it'll be easier.

GREENY: This one's better:

> Golic is a typical idiot jock.

Some we can't even print, not because they're off-color but because they stink.

GOLIC: **Even if they stink, I'd rather read six stinky words:**

> Brevity is the soul of wit.

> Sorry, Golic, but Greeny is right.

> I am too dumb to try.

GREENY: **This was by far the best idea we've ever stolen from *Golf Digest*.**

GOLIC: **If we asked for 600-word essays, how many do you think we would have gotten? Four?**

GREENY: **I still maintain that it's harder to write a good six-word essay. Let me give you an analogy, because I think you're going to agree. Both you and I have a radio show, and we also do television. In other words, we have experience in both mediums. Or media. Whatever. People often ask me which one is more demanding, TV or radio, and I always give them the following answer: It's much *easier* to do radio badly than it is to do television badly; but it is much *harder* to do radio well than it is to do television well. In TV, you have nine million things going on. You can have interesting graphics, good video, whatever. But a radio show, at the end of the day, is simply one person talking into a microphone. That's it. To do that well requires incredible skill, and it's much harder to do than a good television show. Wouldn't you agree?**

GOLIC: **I can't understand you at all. You're an idiot. Radio and television are two completely different animals. We're talking** about words, either 600 of them or only six. Same thing, different amount.

GREENY: But it's so much harder to write six interesting, memorable words. Mike, who are the geniuses of the English language? They are the poets, the songwriters. Think about Paul Simon. Every once in a while I'll be listening to a song of his and hear a line, a short, simple phrase, that conveys a thousand words' worth of emotion. There's a line in "America," which he did when he was with Art Garfunkel:

"Kathy, I'm lost," I said, though I knew she was sleeping.

It's 11 words, not six, but still, with just a few words he's able to draw you a complete picture: They're on a bus, they're both tired, she's sleeping; he calls out to her, says her name, even though he realizes that she won't hear him. Those 11 words convey so much, and more. He doesn't need 600 words to do that. For most people, it would be very hard, maybe impossible. But not for a genius like Paul Simon.

GOLIC: You don't need to be a genius to write a good six-word essay. There were plenty of submissions I liked:

Please replace Greeny with Erin Andrews.

More difficult, but not necessarily harder.

Chargers stink—Norv has to go.

College football needs a playoff system.

He who doesn't understand must learn.

Don't find fault. Find a remedy.

GREENY: That you *liked.* Sure, some are interesting, some are creative, and they're all fun to read, yet most of them aren't memorable. And c'mon, that last one sounds like a fortune cookie. But these might be my top three:

> This makes procrastination very, very easy.

> Mike's right, and Mike is wrong.

> Six words are four too many.

GOLIC: I really like *Mike's right, and Mike is wrong.* Sums up the discussion perfectly.

GREENY: It's pretty clever.

GOLIC: I think it's *genius.*

RULE 4.00: Just because you can't answer a question doesn't mean you're an idiot.

GREENY: I took a philosophy course back in college, and I'll always remember what the professor said in class one day. The only questions worth asking in life, he told us, are the ones we cannot answer.

Every sport asks one very basic question: Who's Number One? And every sport answers it definitively—the Super Bowl, the World Series, March Madness, the NBA championship, the Stanley Cup playoffs. Every sport, that is, except one: college football. Who's Number One? Depends who you ask. Fans of Southern Cal can forever argue that even though they were left out of the national championship game in 2003, the Trojans were the best team in the country that year, and not LSU. The voters of the Associated Press poll thought so, too. What about the 13–0 Auburn Tigers in 2004 when, instead of them, undefeated Oklahoma and USC were picked to play for the BCS title? Boise State and Utah can state their cases for being the best in the country with perfect records in years when the BCS champion was not an undefeated team. Division I football is the only sport that leaves us with several possible answers, so it's the most philosophical of sports.

GOLIC: But we wouldn't need to debate it if they did what every other sport has been able to figure out. Hold a playoff. At the end of the regular season, pick the top four or eight teams and have them settle it not with computer programs or ballots but on the field, where games are meant to be settled.

GREENY: You know, I used to think that way. I grew up in New York and lived and worked in Chicago. By their nature, big cities are pro sports cities. As a kid, my life revolved around the Jets and the Knicks, and my passion for college football just wasn't as strong. Even when I went to college at Northwestern, I wasn't concerned with how USC or Oklahoma were doing. Our big thing was tearing down the goalposts after we beat Northern Illinois. College football should just have a playoff, I thought. But I've got to tell you, now I'm absolutely pumped up for the games every Saturday, from the very first week in September onward. Because of the way they decide a championship, every game is a playoff, and no other sport's regular season is nearly as compelling. I'm a convert now, and I don't want them to have a playoff. I don't.

GOLIC: But a playoff wouldn't end the debate, Greeny. Instead of who's Number One, it would shift to who's Number Six, or Seven, or Eight. The regular season would still be great, so it's not a good reason to keep things the way they are. Any justification for why college football won't structure a playoff system—not can't, *won't*—aren't reasons at all. They're excuses. Student athletes can't take any more time away from the classroom? Stop it. College basketball and Division II and III football manage to figure it out just fine, and their athletes are students, too. The real reason we don't have a playoff is not because the BCS wants to have their championship be a philosophical question. It's money. Before the BCS, the big conferences had agreements in place for guaranteed, multimillion-dollar paydays. We won't have a playoff until college football can find a way to appease the major conferences, because they're not about to leave big money on the table.

GREENY: Regardless of the money, the regular season would not be the same. We're on the edge of our seats from the very first game because a single loss can knock a team out of contention. It's not the end of the world for the Steelers if they lose in Week 5. And midway through the NFL season, you're never trying to figure out who's the second-best team in the NFC or how the Patriots' one loss against the Dolphins measures up against the Colts' one loss against the Broncos. It doesn't matter. They're all going to figure it out in the playoffs, and the champion will be whichever team wins the Super Bowl. It's definitive, sure, but is it more compelling?

The NFL—and all other sports, for that matter—depends on great games. In college football, the discussion is great even when the games are not. If the game is close, great. But even if it's not, you start thinking about how the game's outcome might affect other teams. Who has the advantage now? What's the impact? Even if the game is a dog, endless conversation will come from it, and the discussion is always engrossing.

GOLIC: I still want a good game. I don't want to see an **NFL** game turn into a blowout, but if it does, I'm not crazy enough to say that they should scrap the playoffs.

GREENY: I'm going to bring someone in who's argued with you consistently and who has consistently been right. He's perhaps the best college football analyst in America. He's Mel Kiper, Jr.

MEL KIPER, JR.: Greeny, I agree with you that college football has one of the greatest regular seasons in all of sports.

GREENY: Thanks, Mel.

MEL KIPER, JR.: But I also think it has one of the worst postseasons.

GREENY: You do?

MEL KIPER, JR.: It's all about one game, the BCS championship, and 62 other teams play in bowls that, to me, serve only as consolation prizes. All I care about is changing the system to at least a plus-one game, which we don't currently have.

It's a playoff every week in college football? It's not, because you're not having the matchups that you have in other sports. In college football, you can play against teams that aren't playoff material. Other sports have two playoff teams that are deciding it on the field. With college

One nation, one time zone.

 GREENY: Counting Alaska and Hawaii, we have six time zones in the United States. *Six.* That's way too many. What are we trying to accomplish with them? Why is 7:00 P.M. in Seattle and 7:00 P.M. in New York not the same thing? It all seems very loosey-goosey to me.

Here's what we do: Just have one time zone for everyone, and get on with our lives. And we should all set our clocks to the best time zone of all, Pacific Standard. Why? This is what Sundays are like in Pacific Time: You wake up, have a little breakfast, and—boom!—you're watching football. It's 10 o'clock in the morning and the game is starting. That's what I want. It's fantastic.

 GOLIC: But then you'd have the sun rising at 3:30 in the morning on the East Coast.

GREENY: Okay, who's that affecting, really?

GOLIC: Everyone living on the East Coast.

GREENY: I live on the East Coast. I'm up at 3:30 in the morning. It would be nice to have a little sun then. The important question to ask is how it will affect the farming. My concern is for the farmer, and I just don't know the answer. I need to research this. Do you have a *Farmer's Almanac*?

GOLIC: You're an idiot.

Honolulu

Los Angeles

Chicago

New York

football, you're doing fantasy league stuff—if this, then maybe that . . . or could it be this. Who really knows? It's clearly not the way to settle things, and it's unfortunate.

GREENY: Thanks, Mel, but I say that one man's "unfortunate" is another man's "thank goodness."

GOLIC: No, Mel's right. To fans of those teams that feel left out, whether it be USC or Auburn or Boise State, if you gave them a choice between having a playoff or getting screwed, which one do you think they would choose? Everybody would take the playoff.

GREENY: Not everyone, Mike. There's a certain beauty in the lack of an answer. In the immediacy of the moment, maybe you'd say yes, but not everything in life has an answer or a definitive ending. College football is like the ending of *The Sopranos*, perhaps the most talked-about season finale in television history outside of *M*A*S*H*. If you saw Tony Soprano get whacked while he's sitting in the diner, you might get

your initial fill. But in a couple of days, what is there to talk about? Nothing. The way they ended the series—Tony is eating onion rings, there's a sense of foreboding, and then the screen abruptly goes to black—now that's something you have to discuss. It's not decided for you. What happens to Tony? The answer can be anything you want it to be.

GOLIC: Here's the thing about Tony Soprano, and I don't mean to break it to you: He's fake, okay? There is no Tony Soprano. He was a role played by James Gandolfini. They're fake people, Greeny. And the ending stunk because it was a cop-out. I hated it. If sports ended the way *The Sopranos* did, you'd be the first one screaming at the TV screen. Let's say it's Game Seven of the World Series and the score is tied in the bottom of the ninth, full count, bases loaded. The pitcher is about to start his windup and suddenly . . . both teams walk off the field! Game over. No conclusion. Great stuff, right? You get to make up your own mind about who won the game.

When some people start thinking, they overthink. You're making a complete fool out of yourself.

GREENY: I'm not suggesting we pull the plug in the middle of a game. Do you agree with me, at least, that college football has a great season?

GOLIC: I would say that's true, yes.

GREENY: But you're not sold on the ending, right?

GOLIC: I am not sold, at all.

GREENY: I have the perfect analogy for this. First, let's compare college football to, say, college basketball. The college football season is unbelievably good. You don't want to miss a single weekend because you never know what's going to happen next, all this craziness, and then you get to how they determine the last game, and maybe it's a little disappointing for you. College basketball is just the opposite. When you think about their regular season, you can take it or leave it, but then the tournament starts and for three weekends in March, you're absolutely glued to it. It's all about the ending. So here's my analogy: I recently read two books, and I had a vastly different experience with each one. The first was called *The Ghost,* written by Robert Harris. I hadn't enjoyed reading a book this much for as long as I can remember, but then at the end it really fell apart for me. The next book I picked up was *The Abstinence Teacher* by Tom Perrotta. I thought it was really boring. But when I got to the last 30 pages, it was magnificent. The ending was tremendous. My question to you is, would you rather read something that you enjoy for 270 pages but then the last 30 disappoint you, or the one that you loved for the last 30 pages but the first 270 weren't so great? Which one is better?

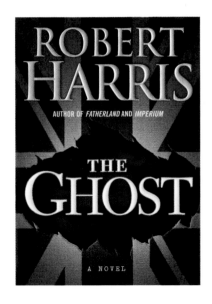

GOLIC: Give me a great ending every time. I'd feel let down if I got to the end and it wasn't good. End it on a high note.

GREENY: But you probably wouldn't be able to sit through it to get to the end. Everyone would choose the other one.

GOLIC: Not me.

GREENY: I've just discovered the most important rule of all: It's my job to convince you that I'm right.

GOLIC: Well, good luck with that. Remember, "Mike's right, and Mike is wrong."

GREENY: Exactly. **M**&**M**

RULE 4.08

Watch your blind side.

He was the most feared defensive lineman named Golic in the history of the game . . . at least after his brother Bob. The complete story of an NFL career, as told in 11 $\frac{1}{2}$ sacks:

2

In December 1989, Phil Simms was sacked by Mike Golic and fumbled, which set up the game-winning touchdown for the Eagles. Thank you, Mike Golic.

3

On September 23, 1990, Jim Everett of the Los Angeles Rams was the quarterback in a football game. Mike Golic had no choice but to sack him.

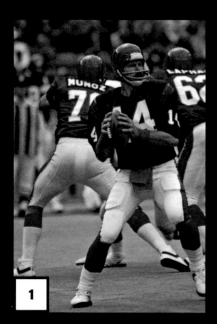

1

Ken Anderson had played for 16 seasons in the NFL when Mike Golic sacked him in November 1986. Later, Anderson retired.

4 and 5

Where were you on September 15, 1991? Probably not in Texas Stadium, sacking Troy Aikman twice in one game. That was Mike Golic.

5$\frac{1}{2}$

Steve Young was never the same after Mike Golic recorded a half-sack against him in October 1991.

6½

In his playing days, Mike Golic ate quarterbacks like Neil Lomax for breakfast. He also sacked him once.

7½

Tom Tupa was an NFL quarterback, so Mike Golic sacked him.

8½

Mike Golic terrorized Cardinals quarterbacks. On one play, Kent Graham was no exception.

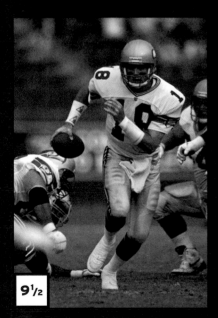

9½

Mike Golic couldn't resist sacking Stan Gelbaugh one time.

10½

Quarterback Babe Laufenberg was no match for Mike Golic.

11½

Marc Wilson was sacked 210 times in his career. Had it not been for Mike Golic, he would have been sacked only 209 times.

OVER-
TIME

RULE
5.36:

A House Without a Baseball Glove Is Not a Home.

GREENY: There's a diner near our home where I often take my kids out for dinner. They always order their favorite, scrambled eggs and French fries. We go on Saturday mornings for breakfast, too, but when we do, they're not allowed to order French fries. Why? Because we don't eat French fries at breakfast. That's our rule.

So we're at the diner one morning, and we're all having eggs only, like we're supposed to, when my daughter, Nikki, turns to me and says, "Daddy, it's breakfast time, but that man is eating French fries. Go tell him he shouldn't." I look over and see a guy reading the newspaper and eating sunny-side-up eggs with a side of fries. He catches me staring at him and I turn away quickly.

Now, am I going to have to get up and lecture a complete stranger on not eating French fries for breakfast? How do I explain this to Nikki?

 GOLIC: Simple. You tell her that this is a rule in your house, but that's it. You have your rules, and the man at the diner has his rules.

GREENY: Well, the guy really *shouldn't* be eating French fries, Mike. It's nine in the morning. Would you want to wake up and eat a burger or a Caesar salad right away?

GOLIC: Sure, if it's available. Maybe a bacon cheeseburger. With fries, too. You should let your kids have some French fries with their eggs at breakfast. I'm not telling you to buy a deep fryer or anything, but if you're out and your kids want French fries, what's the harm? People have hash browns for breakfast. If you mash them up and shape them like a bunch of French fries, what's the difference? Listen to me, because I know my food: French fries are okay in the morning.

GREENY: Nikki doesn't know hash browns exist. And we don't eat French fries at breakfast, period. There is honor in our house.

But I've put the idea in my daughter's head that *nobody* can eat French fries in the morning. She sometimes gets so concerned that she alerts the waitresses when she sees someone breaking the rule. I actually like that she's taken our rules to heart. My son, on the other hand, is not so completely sold. I was putting him to bed one night, and I was telling him a little bedtime story. Stephen is absolutely obsessed with Superman—there's nothing he's

interested in that doesn't have something to do with Superman—so I tell him a story about how he's actually Superman saving the neighborhood dogs from bad guys. I finish—a happy ending, Stevie saves every dog—and wish him a good night and reach to turn off the light.

"Good night, stupid-butt Daddy!" he says.

I stop him right there. His little friends have taught him this term, "stupid butt," and now he won't stop using it. "We don't say that," I tell him.

Here's the problem, though: He looks me right in the eye and says, "But Daddy, you said it on the radio."

GOLIC: This is when you throw him the line, "Look up. You see that roof? It's mine. You're living under *my* roof, friend."

GREENY: I'm going to throw him out on the streets?

GOLIC: You tell him that you're the parent, and you get to say those things but as a kid, he can't. If that doesn't work, you go to Plan B.

GREENY: Plan B?

GOLIC: Soap.

GREENY: What do you mean, soap? We wash the child. He's clean.

GOLIC: No, no, no. You want him to stop saying those words? Wash the inside of his mouth with a bar of soap. Just put a little bar in his mouth, enough to get the bad taste in there. Next time he says "stupid butt," he knows the soap is coming. I'm telling you, he won't be saying "stupid butt" much longer. It worked on all three of my kids. Jake actually enjoyed it, though, so I had to get the soap a little deeper to get the full effect. You know what I'm talking about?

GREENY: *Oy vey.*

GOLIC: I'm telling you, so many people do this. I'm not saying you make them eat a bar of soap for dinner. A little soap in the mouth.

GREENY: What are we, in a Charles Dickens novel?

RULE 5.15: If you're trying to be friends, stop it.

GREENY: You have some explaining to do.

GOLIC: I do?

GREENY: Yes. The other day, we did the radio show in the morning, and then I stayed to do *SportsCenter* that night. I was in the office all afternoon. At one point, I was sitting at my desk and I noticed there was a voice mail on my cell phone. Someone had called. I checked the message, and it was from you, reminding me of a meeting we were trying to set up for the following week. On the message, it sounded like you were tired and trying to relax after a long day. Up to this point, everything was completely normal and ordinary until— and I don't know if you realized it or not—you forgot to hang up.

RULE 5.16

Everyone looks like somebody else.

GREENY: The very first time I anchored *SportsCenter*—on a Saturday in October 1996—it was a dream come true for me. I was so excited and, afterward, a little relieved, too. I was pretty sure that everything went relatively well, and I took my then-girlfriend Stacy (now my wife) out to dinner to celebrate.

We sit down and the waiter comes over with our menus. "I'm a big sports fan," he tells me. "It's a pleasure to have you in the restaurant."

Wow. Stacy and I can't believe it. *SportsCenter* is popular, but after doing just one show, people are recognizing me. How great is this?

Throughout the dinner, the waiter keeps asking me questions about sports. Do I think the Braves have a chance to win the World Series? Who's going to win the Heisman, Jake Plummer or Danny Wuerffel? It was amazing. All of a sudden, I'm somewhat famous. Stacy doesn't follow sports closely, but I can tell she's impressed, maybe even a little proud of me.

After dessert, the waiter comes over with the check. As he's putting it down on the table, he says, "It's been a pleasure to serve you, Mr. Levy. Thank you very much for coming in tonight."

Stacy looks at me, completely baffled. "Mr. *Levy*?"

The waiter thought I was Steve Levy, and right in front of my girl, too.

GOLIC: I did?

GREENY: Whatever you did, you didn't hang up the phone, and as the message went on I could hear the conversation you were having with your wife. Chris was obviously very close to the phone, her voice as clear as yours, and the tone was heading in a direction that, to be perfectly honest, was making me feel uncomfortable. Simply put, I was starting to freak out.

I realized that I had reached a crossroads: Do I continue to listen, or do I hang up?

GOLIC: You listened.

GREENY: No way. I deleted it, 337-ed as fast as I could. I thought that if this thing is going where I think it's going, I'm never going to survive the experience. What the hell was going on over there?

GOLIC: Well, yeah, ya know . . .

GREENY: What's the matter with you? Were you or were you not lying down in bed when you left me the message?

GOLIC: I was.

GREENY: I heard someone say *It's not moving.*

GOLIC: Okay, what happened was this: I left you the message about the meeting, and then I threw down the phone, and Chris and I were talking. My knee was injured, it was hurting, and I had it propped up on the bed under a couple of pillows. I was trying to move it, and I said, "It's not moving right."

GREENY: When I heard that something wasn't moving right, I had to hang up. I just couldn't listen. Right before that, I heard you and Chris talking about picking the kids up at school the next day and running errands. There was a strange detached quality to the way the two of you were speaking, and I've been married long enough to know that you can have that conversation and perform other, marital-relation things at the same time, believe you me. I know what was going on.

GOLIC: It was a perfectly innocent moment. I was just tired.

GREENY: Put yourself in my shoes. You get a message from a co-worker who accidentally doesn't hang up the phone and is about to get intimate with his wife. What's the rule here? What do you do?

GOLIC: Oh, I'm listening. Totally.

GREENY: And would you play it for other people at work the next day?

GOLIC: Of course. The more, the better. And I'm putting a stopwatch to it.

GREENY: Lucky for you I deleted it.

GOLIC: Nothing happened, I swear, which is more than I can say for you when you "borrowed" my car.

GREENY: There was no funny business going on in your car while it was under my jurisdiction, at least that I'm aware of. Here's the thing: For a dinner in New York City, you wanted to drive to my house, leave your car, get a car service to drive you and your wife into New York, and then return the next day to pick up your car. Who does that?

GOLIC: Your house is closer to the city than mine is.

GREENY: Right. I forget that you live in a little shack in the woods somewhere. Anyway, I said okay, and you and Chris drove over and left the car in the driveway. But as you're leaving, you ask me if you should leave the keys in it in case I need to move it. What? I'm not sure what you thought might happen. Do we have alternate-side-of-the-street parking in my driveway?

GOLIC: It's a common courtesy. You never know.

GREENY: Maybe, but to me, it's like asking a five-year-old if he wants to play with matches. The second you leave—you weren't even out of sight, the car service hadn't made the left turn out of the driveway—I'm behind the wheel, revving her up for a little spin, and soon I'm zipping around the streets of suburban Connecticut. It corners like it's on rails . . . I'm Joel in *Risky Business*, taking the parents' car out for a joyride. I'm driving your U-boat, thinking, *"Porsche, there is no substitute."*

GOLIC: Which would have been okay if you left it at that, but when I wake up the next morning in my hotel room and turn on the radio . . .

> **GREENY:** I have Golic's car, and I've driven it to work. I've got Golic's car right outside in the parking lot, and if anyone is interested in driving it, I've got the keys here.
>
> **GUEST HOST TREY WINGO:** Golic gave you the keys?
>
> **GREENY:** Golic gave me the keys, and I certainly hope that his insurance payments are up-to-date, because I've never been accused of being a good driver. That has never happened. In just the years that I have been doing this show, I have had two accidents, I have had tires blow out, and I had to have someone come get me on the highway twice. I had to go to traffic school for three hours because they were going to take my license away.
>
> **TREY WINGO:** I had to go to traffic school, too!
>
> **GREENY:** Great, you want to drive Golic's car? Here, the keys are in my pocket. Any of our listeners interested in taking a spin in Golic's car, just let us know. The Mike and Mike inbox is open.
>
> —MIKE AND MIKE IN THE MORNING,
> July 25, 2006

GREENY: In my defense, I'd like to point out that all the scratches were relatively minor.

GOLIC: The tires were completely bald!

RULE 5.21

Good advice comes when you least expect it.

GREENY: The first time I met Lou Holtz, we taped a *SportsCenter* segment together. Afterward, we were walking down the hall on our way out of the studio. Holtz walks very fast, and I'm chasing just to keep up with him, trying to make any small talk that comes to mind. Out of nowhere, Holtz stops and turns to me.

"How many kids you got?" he asks.

"I have two," I tell him, a little surprised. "They're, you know, little kids."

He looks me straight in the eye. "The best thing you can do for them? Make sure that, every day, they know how much you love their mother."

And with that, Lou Holtz walked down the hall and out the door.

RULE 5.22

Fruit is not a dessert.

GREENY: I disagree. To me, some nice fresh fruit, sliced and served on a plate with some strawberries and maybe some raspberries, is as good a dessert as anything.

GOLIC: That's not dessert. It's a snack.

GREENY: As a post-dinner dish, it's a lovely dessert. You have a nice little fruit plate with a glass of red wine, and it's phenomenal. You'll walk away from the table after dinner and not feel stuffed. Trust me. You'll feel good.

GOLIC: Thanks, but I feel good after a big bowl of ice cream.

GREENY: The thing is, you dropping off your car at my house is one of the few times that our lives have intersected outside of work. Except for attending a work-related function or taking the show on the road, we've spent practically zero time together outside of the office. Our personal lives are by and large completely separate from our work lives—more by accident than by design—and, in all candor, I think that's the secret to getting along well with the people you work with.

For some reason, people who work together often feel they should be spending time together outside the office, as well. "We should hang out . . . We need to get the families together . . . We should get our wives together . . . We need our kids to play together . . . We need to plan a vacation together." No, you *don't*. You really don't. There is absolutely no reason for that. In fact, it's a huge mistake. Every job, no matter what it is, has its challenges. Any number of things can happen, but the biggest challenge is not allowing the personal stuff between co-workers to interfere with work. Those issues can lead to personal resentment, and can really eat away at a work relationship. But they can't enter the equation if they don't exist.

GOLIC: You're making it sound like we avoid each other.

GREENY: Not at all. It's just worked out that way. A lot of people will interpret it to mean that we're not friends. That's not true. You can have a close personal relationship with someone at work without having all the other stuff from outside crowding in on it. It's unnecessary. In many ways, we have the *perfect* working relationship.

GOLIC: Really? Because I was just avoiding you.

RULE 5.23: If you're in charge of people you normally aren't in charge of, don't act like you're in charge of them.

GREENY: Are we in charge of people? As far as I can tell, we report to the suits, and our staff at *Mike and Mike* reports to the suits, too, so we're in charge of *nobody*. I've been in this business for 20 years and I'm still pressing random buttons on the copy machine to try to clear a paper jam. Why? Because I'm not in charge of anybody.

GOLIC: The copier's not that difficult. And even though we're not in charge of anyone at work, we get to be managers, literally—for the All-Star Legends & Celebrities softball game, first in Yankee Stadium in 2008 and then last year at Busch Stadium. How cool is that? You were in charge of all these Hall of Famers and big stars—Billy Crystal, Chris Rock, Dave Winfield, Nelly, Wade Boggs, Spike Lee—but you and I should have a little talk about it.

GREENY: I don't want to hear it from you. I was in charge. I managed my *tuchus* off, my team won, and I can give you a million examples of how in charge I was. The only person who made no pretense of listening to me was Bob Knight. Whenever I tried to talk to him, he would stare me down until I cowered. You know how you can stare at a dog long enough, and he'll back down? That was Bob Knight's tactic with me. Before the first pitch, I walked over to him in the dugout to discuss my plan for victory.

"Hi, Coach," I said. "Here's where I'd like you to play today." He stared at me, very intently, and didn't say a word.

"Okay, Coach, let me rephrase that: Where would *you* like to play?"

First base, he told me. End of discussion.

GOLIC: Right. You're normally not in charge of Bob Knight, so if you *are* in charge of him for a softball game, don't act like you are. Because I spoke to Bob Knight after the game, and he told me he doesn't want to play for you anymore. He wants to play for me.

GREENY: I thought he *liked* playing for me.

GOLIC: Ha.

GREENY: Listen, I was in charge. This was one serious softball game. Billy Bob Thornton was taking it seriously, too. At one point, Ozzie Smith made one of his unbelievable, Wizard of Oz diving plays at short and quickly flipped the ball over to second for the force. Billy Bob Thornton was my second baseman. He was so stunned by Ozzie's play—everyone was stunned—that he was nowhere near the bag to take the throw. I remember that you were the runner going to second, and it was the only reason you were safe on the play.

After the inning was over, Billy Bob came over and said, "Sorry about that, Skip." That's how seriously he was taking the game. And he called me Skip, because I was the skipper. I was in charge.

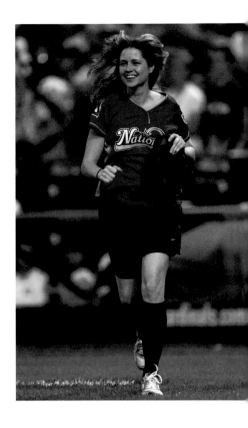

GOLIC: And what did you tell Billy Bob Thornton? Did you jump on him and read him the riot act? *Noooooo.* You cowered, curled up in the fetal position, and sucked your thumb.

GREENY: Not true. What I said to him was, "You know what, Billy Bob? I was as stunned at the play Ozzie made as you were. Don't worry about it."

GOLIC: But you were stunned *the entire game.* There was one play where you hit a weak grounder, put your head down, ran as fast as you could to first, and then looked around like a moron, wondering why you were safe. You sorta forgot to notice that you had forced Jenna Fischer from *The Office* at second, and boy, did she let you have it in the clubhouse after the game. Nice going, Skippy.

GREENY: It's Skip. You know, I wanted to get a hit so badly. Twice I hit the ball to Brian Littrell, the Backstreet Boy. No knock on him—he's a very good ballplayer, and a nice guy, too—but if I'm going to make an out, I want a Hall of Famer making the play: Paul Molitor, Goose Gossage, George Brett. It was a thrill to meet George Brett, actually, and at Yankee Stadium, too, the site of his famous reaction after hitting the pine-tar home run. But have you noticed that George Brett has a new tactic these days when he gets upset? He whispers.

GOLIC: He whispers when he's mad?

WHEN WE COME BACK ON PAGE 230, WE'LL TELL YOU WHAT GEORGE BRETT HAS IN COMMON WITH TEDDY ROOSEVELT.

Wife and Wife in the Morning

29 Questions for the Spouses of Mike and Mike

SG: Stacy Steponate Greenberg
CG: Chris Golic

Hometown?

SG: Chicago, Illinois
CG: Palos Hills, Illinois, a suburb of Chicago

Education?

SG: Master's in Integrated Marketing, Northwestern University, Evanston, Illinois
CG: Bachelor of Business Administration, St. Mary's College, Notre Dame, Indiana

When did you meet your Mike?

SG: Introduced by a mutual friend at a health club in Chicago who made the Northwestern University connection. Mike likes to tell people that he asked me out while he was lifting serious weights. Yeah, like *that* would happen.
CG: First day of school, freshman year. He was coming out of the dorm with a bunch of other guys, and we all went to a freshman mixer at the Joyce Center.

First date?

SG: Dinner at Brasserie Jo in Chicago. I drank way too much wine, which is probably what made me like him.
CG: An official date? Sophomore year, we went to a dance together, but we kissed freshman year by the old Log Cabin on campus. We started going out senior year, although we kind of started toward the end of junior year.

How did you spend your first New Year's Eve together?

SG: He sang the *Partridge Family* songs.
CG: We're not big New Year's people. We went to a restaurant, and I was begging to leave by 10:00 P.M.

Your most recent New Year's Eve?

SG: We actually hung out with David Cassidy.
CG: At home with friends.

How did your Mike propose?

SG: He had big plans to propose on Valentine's Day, but he cannot—I repeat, *cannot*—keep a secret to save his life. He proposed to me on February 13. Get the picture?

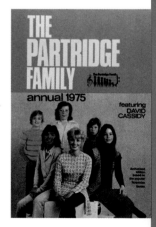

CG: It was the worst-kept secret, and there was no wow factor to it. He called me the day he picked up the engagement ring and said, "Chris, I've got it. Do you want to know what it looks like?" He took me to a Michael Stanley Band concert, and while we were sitting in the car in the parking lot of the Rosemont Horizon, he handed me the ring. It drives him nuts with regret when he thinks about it now.

How was the wedding?

SG: Fun and easy. No bad drama. When it was time for speeches, Mike made a sweet, funny, and touching toast.
CG: We were married in Sacred Heart Roman Catholic church in Palos Hills and held the reception at the Drake in Oak Brook. Every guy in the wedding party changed into jammer shorts and gym shoes. They had squirt guns, too.

The honeymoon?

SG: Two weeks in Morocco and Spain started with Mike trying to explain to the customs officer (who spoke only Arabic) why his suitcase was filled with cans of tuna fish, Pop-Tarts, and juice boxes.
CG: A week and a half in Aruba. When I got off the plane, I started not feeling well, and it went downhill from there. For the first half of the vacation, I was sick in bed,

and Mike was doing everything by himself. Scuba lessons, gambling, everything.

Children?

SG: Three if you include Mike.
CG: Two sons, one daughter.

Pets?

SG: Hermit crabs. As Mike proudly states, they don't carry salmonella.
CG: Three dogs and one cat.

How often do you listen to the show?

SG: Never.
CG: Always.

His drink of choice?

SG: Red wine.
CG: Beer, any brand.

Mike's most annoying habit is . . .

SG: When he comes home from work, he'll stand at the door and announce, "Honey, I'm back and better than ever!"

CG: We can't have HBO in the house anymore because he would watch the same movie 20 times a week. *Road House* with Patrick Swayze. *The Mummy. Armageddon.* If there was a Mummy channel on cable, he'd subscribe to it.

His pet peeve?

SG: Mike doesn't like people, animals, or sharing.

CG: Mike hates it when I complain about his driving, especially while he's driving.

His favorite meal?

SG: Italian food, but someone has to cook it for him. He can't cook anything. Tops on his list is insalata caprese and then grilled chicken in white wine with mushrooms and artichokes.

CG: A peanut-butter-and-jelly sandwich that has to have more than two slices of bread.

The worst gift Mike ever gave you?

SG: For my first birthday that we celebrated together, cheesy lingerie. Never worn.

CG: For Mother's Day, he went with the boys to Sharper Image and bought me a massage chair. I used it twice, maybe. It went straight into the boys' room. When Mike comes home from work, he goes upstairs and falls asleep in it.

His secret passion . . .

SG: He skinny-dips in our pool when he thinks no one can see him. We've lost a lot of baby-sitters.

CG: His feet. Every night before he goes to sleep—at home or on the road—he'll sit down on the edge of the bed and moisturize his feet with Origins lotion. He says that he likes his feet to feel soft.

If you could burn one thing in his closet . . .

SG: Already done. There's nothing in his closet I didn't put there.

CG: Maybe his green Eddie Bauer sweatshirt. It's really old. He sometimes wears it to bed.

His strangest friend?

SG: Most of his friends are imaginary.

CG: Greeny.

A movie that made Mike cry . . .

SG: *High School Musical 3.* He wasn't ready to say goodbye.

CG: Definitely *Brian's Song*. He cries during a lot of movies. Not sobbing, but he'll tear up.

His favorite fruit?

SG: **Mango.**
CG: **Pear.**

Mike is addicted to . . .

SG: *Seinfeld*, **golf, ginger candies, golf, massages, golf.**
CG: *The National Enquirer.* **Also, Nicolas Cage movies.**

Automatic or stick?

SG: **Oh dear lord, he can barely drive at all.**
CG: **Automatic.**

Dopp-kit item he won't leave home without?

SG: **Garnier facial wipes.**
CG: **Nothing. He's okay walking out of the house with just a $5 bill in his pocket.**

Strangest thing in his medicine cabinet?

SG: **Lip gloss.**
CG: **For deodorant, he uses Secret. Not mine—he has his own. It's his favorite.**

His greatest fear?

SG: **Being eaten by anything: sharks, lions, large dogs.**
CG: **Except for throwing out first pitches at ballparks, Mike is fearless.**

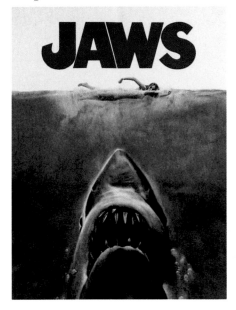

On his iPod, you'll find . . .

SG: **Barry Manilow's "Tryin' To Get the Feeling." The entire album.**
CG: **He listens to everything, from Johnny Mathis to Taylor Swift. He loves singer-songwriters especially, like Gordon Lightfoot and Harry Chapin.**

His secret crush?

SG: **Bill Belichick. I'm not kidding.**
CG: **Kathy Ireland, back when the *Sports Illustrated* swimsuit issue was all the rage.**

If Mike wasn't doing the radio show, he'd be . . .

SG: **A Broadway musical star.**
CG: **An assistant coach at Notre Dame.**

GREENY: He whispers. During yet another disappointing summer for the Royals, Brett was asked about the criticism surrounding the team's manager. George Brett's reply:

```
"!!#&!! you and !!#&!! them. Believe me, every
sports guy in town has never interviewed for a
manager's job. You know why? Because there's 30
teams in major league baseball
    (quieter) no one's ever called these guys to
manage, have they?
        (even quieter) No one's ever called them to be the
        general manager. Why? Because they don't know what
        they're talking about sometimes,
            (whispering) they don't know what they're talking about
            sometimes. And I'm sick and tired of listening to it, okay? I'm
            sick and tired of listening to it . . ."
```

GOLIC: Wow! You know, I love it when he starts getting quiet.

GREENY: You're a yeller, right? When you get excited about something, you yell.

GOLIC: Yes I do.

GREENY: The truth is, yelling can be very effective, but only up to a point. If you yell too much, you run the risk of becoming the boy who cried wolf. When you were a kid and your parents got mad at you and yelled, you knew how to deal with it. It's when they got quiet that you went hiding under the bed.

GOLIC: When they're angry *and* calm about it, it's like they're insane.

GREENY: I remember one time, I was a little kid, and we were up at our family's vacation house. My brother and I were outside having a water fight with the garden hose. My mother had gotten all dressed up to go out for a fancy dinner, and when she walked out of the house to the car, I shouted, "Hey, Mom!" and—*squirt!*—I got her. I mean, she was *drenched.*

She didn't yell. Instead, she got very, very quiet. And I was terrified.

If George Brett is singlehandedly trying to bring back the angry whisper, I'm all for it. Speak softly and carry a big stick. In my opinion, George Brett can do very little wrong. We're all influenced by our own experience, and I've always had a soft spot for the players who were the best when I was a little kid, just starting to understand and appreciate the sport. To me, they're on a pedestal as among the greatest of all time—players like Joe Morgan, Reggie Jackson, Carlton Fisk. And George Brett, Hall of Fame third-baseman and 1980 A.L. MVP. Brett is great after the comma.

GOLIC: After the comma?

GREENY: Yes. You know how you'll read a person's name, then a comma, and then some descriptive phrase? George Brett has really great things after his comma. Billy Bob Thornton, Academy Award–winning actor. Great comma. Steve Young, Hall of Fame quarterback. Great comma. Tom Hanks, nominated for five Oscars for Best Actor and winner of two. *Phenomenal* comma. The key to life is having something good after your comma.

GOLIC: What would we have after our commas?

GREENY: There's really nothing after my comma. You, on the other hand, have several nice commas. Mike Golic, former NFL player. Nice comma. Or Mike Golic, captain of the 1984 Notre Dame football team. Very cool comma. What am I? I'm Mike Greenberg. That's it.

GOLIC: We should think of something for your comma.

GREENY: I've got nothing. I asked my wife, and she drew a blank.

GOLIC: What about Mike Greenberg, Wiggles fan?

GREENY: I guess that's it.

RULE 5.33: Any story becomes 43 percent funnier if someone gets hit in the nuts.

GREENY: Do you realize that most mishaps happen in or around the home?

GOLIC: Do I ever.

GREENY: What happened?

GOLIC: A few years ago, my sons were getting ready for football season—Mike was going to be a sophomore and the starting center, and Jake a freshman. So we're practicing. I try to work everyone into the drills: Mike will be working on his snapping and his steps from the center position; Jake will play tight end and will flex out like a wide receiver to work on his routes. I'll be the quarterback. I ask my wife, Chris, to help out and give her a hand dummy. I ask her to hold the dummy and stand in to represent where the nose tackle would be.

First play, I have Jake do an out route, and I want Mike to make like it's a run wide right—pop the center and then go upfield to block the safety. And we're ready to go.

I do a little cadence thing, and Mike snaps the ball. I take three steps back, see Jake run his out, and then . . . then I see Mike, my 15-year-old-son, absolutely *destroy* his mother with a block, catching her with a hand shiver that jolts her world.

My wife goes ass-over-teakettle, flipping backward, her sunglasses flying though the air. I see her roll on the ground several times before she comes to a stop, completely motionless.

RULE 5.34

Throw paper.

ERIK KUSELIAS: Life's about getting an edge wherever you can. Would you believe that in Rock, Paper, Scissors, most men throw rock 70 percent of the time? Well, not exactly—I just had Liam and Joaquin play a hundred rounds, and Liam threw rock 70 times. Whatever the exact number is, remember that most guys throw rock; it must be a macho thing. Throw paper, and you just might be a step ahead of the competition. Good luck.

Running his out route, Jake turns around to see his mother flying backward through the air. He comes running over to help her. Mike, who just crushed his mother, is downfield. He's completely oblivious and still blocking an imaginary safety.

I try to help my wife get to her feet, but she's still wobbly. "My God, honey, are you all right?"

Mike finally looks back and sees his mother sprawled out on the ground. Her head is spinning. I turned to my son. "Mike, what were you thinking? I said take a step, *pop,* and go. I didn't say *destroy.*"

Mike stares at me blankly. No "I'm sorry" . . . No "I didn't mean to" . . .

"I thought she was going to stand a little tougher, Dad," he says.

It was the last time that Chris played nose tackle.

GREENY: Was she all right?

GOLIC: She was fine after a while. Just rub some dirt on it.

GREENY: You know, you live in a full-contact world. I've heard you mention that, from time to time, you'll wrestle with your sons. Why do I think that every argument at the Golic household is settled by a steel-cage death match? Little Sydney is trying to pin you because she wants an extra 50 cents a week in her allowance. I would last two minutes in your family.

That said, as a father, I've discovered that children can indeed be dangerous. Other people's children? Even more dangerous. My two nephews came over to visit once. They were eight and four at the time. Eric, who's

Dress right.

GREENY: The first professional fight I ever covered as a reporter was Evander Holyfield versus Larry Holmes at Caesars Palace in Las Vegas. I was 24 years old at the time, and I flew out with my father. The plan was that I'd report on the fight, and then my dad and I would spend a couple of days together.

We land in Vegas, and the airline loses my luggage, so we check into the hotel and wait. There's a pre-fight press conference I need to get to, but I still don't have any of my clothes. My dad lends me his tennis shorts, which are so big on me that I have to wear a belt to keep them from falling down. I put on my dress shirt and a pair of dress shoes, because it's all I have. Why I didn't go out and buy some new clothes, I don't know. The airline kept saying that they would deliver my suitcase to me at the hotel in time, and I believed them.

So off I go to the press conference wearing a dress shirt, a pair of white tennis shorts with a black leather belt, and dress shoes with no socks.

It felt like the longest afternoon of my life. I was asked to show my press pass maybe 20 times that day, and I sat there helplessly during the entire press conference as the other reporters whispered to each other and avoided coming anywhere near me.

Afterward, I see George Foreman standing outside the main room doing a one-on-one interview with a reporter. Foreman sees me and stops in mid-sentence. He walks over and eyes me up and down.

"What are you doing wearing *that*?" he asks me.

I start to tell him how the airline had lost my luggage and that I was out here with my father and these are actually his shorts, but as I'm saying this, I realize, Jeez, it's *George Foreman*, Olympic gold medalist, former heavyweight champion of the world, the man who fought Muhammad Ali in the Rumble in the Jungle. There's no way I'm going to explain away the fact that I look like a complete lunatic. So I just stop talking.

George Foreman shakes his head and, without saying a word, walks away.

My first professional fight, and also my last.

eight, is a crazy sports fan, so I say to him, "C'mon, let's go have a little catch." He goes to the car and gets two mitts and a ball.

GOLIC: He went to the car?

GREENY: These are my in-laws. Eric went to his parents' car.

GOLIC: You didn't use your own mitt?

GREENY: No. Why?

GOLIC: Don't you have a mitt at your house?

GREENY: I don't know what became of the mitt I owned when I was a kid. Somewhere along the line, I managed to lose it.

GOLIC: How can you not have a mitt in your house? Usually, you go over someone's house, they have mitts. Everyone has a mitt— it's what makes your house a home. Even better is two mitts— someone comes over, you grab the mitts and go play a game of catch in the backyard. That's a nice thing to do, just the two of you.

GREENY: Well, we managed to do that because my eight-year-old nephew had the forethought to travel with mitts. So we're having a catch, we're throwing the ball, feeling pretty good. He's pitching on his Little League team, so he says, "Uncle Michael, I want to throw a few pitches." We're right out of the swimming pool, okay? We've all been swimming, so I'm wearing nothing but a pair of swimming trunks.

GOLIC: This story is getting kind of complicated.

GREENY: How complicated is it? We're having a catch, wearing bathing suits. We make a little home plate, and I march off 40 feet, which is how far the mound is in his league. I crouch down and he throws a few. We're having a good time. Then it happens—he short-hops me, and I don't get the mitt down quite fast enough. The pitch hits the ground, and on the uprise—bam!

GOLIC: Oh no.

GREENY: Like an *uppercut.* I have not felt pain like that in a long, long time. I go down. Straight down.

GOLIC: Did you scream?

GREENY: I yelped, and then I'm rolling on the ground. Eric comes running over. "Oh no, Uncle Michael! Did it get you in the knee?" Now, I don't know what he knows or doesn't know, but in the moment, I don't have the will to explain it to him. I'm in full flux. I'm in a state of complete panic.

"Is it your knee?" Eric asks again.

I'm barely able to talk, but I manage a yes, because I don't know what else to tell him. "Is it bleeding?" he asks me.

GOLIC: He really thinks that he pinged you on the knee.

GREENY: Fine by me. I manage to get up to my feet and limp over to the pool area, collapsing onto a beach chair. I swear to you, I did not move for an hour

You live, you learn.

TIM KURKJIAN: When I was 15 years old, I took a sociology class in high school. We would meet at the library in groups of four—three very attractive girls, and me—to learn about different cultures. During one class, the subject of circumcision came up, and honest to God, I didn't know what circumcision was. I turned to Tricia and very naively asked her what the word meant.

"Stop joking around," she said dismissively.

"Tricia, I don't know what it is," I said. I was starting to get a little annoyed with her. "Please explain it to me."

"I can't, Timmy . . . I'm a girl." And that was the end of that.

After class, I came home and looked up the word in the dictionary.

```
Circumcision (n): 1. The act of circumcising;
esp. a Jewish rite performed on male infants
as a sign of inclusion in the Jewish religious
community. 2. The surgical removal of the
foreskin from the penis.
```

Oh no. And I was asking those poor girls!

At my 20-year high school reunion, I ran into Tricia. I was hoping that, in the swirl of high school, she'd forgotten about that afternoon in sociology class at the library. She remembered it like yesterday.

and 45 minutes. The kids went swimming, everyone gets up, they shower, eat dinner, but I never moved out of that chair.

GOLIC: Might have saved you if you had your own mitt.

GREENY: It might have, yes.

Rule 5.39: End on a good note.

GREENY: What do you mean, "end"?

GOLIC: I think we're starting to run out of pages, Greeny. It's probably time for us to wrap this up.

GREENY: Wrap it up? But I still have to go over my plan on how to revamp baseball's wild-card format. And the rules for a good mani-pedi. And I definitely want to answer any critics who've trashed us in the past. That's a rule: Never answer your critics until you get to write a book.

GOLIC: Hold on. We should probably leave that alone, at least for now. Whenever athletes get into it with their critics, they almost always come across as either really spoiled or really insane. They're better off just biting their lip, counting to 10, and getting on with life.

The same should go for us, too, I think. And pedicures? We should definitely leave your feet out of this.

GREENY: So I guess this is the end.

GOLIC: I think so.

GREENY: But we'll be on the air again in the morning, back and better than ever?

GOLIC: You bet.

GREENY: Good. You know, this probably gives us enough time for a quick manicure, me and you. What do you say?

GOLIC: You're an idiot. **M&M**

RULE 5.40: THE BEST PART OF SPORTS BOOKS? OLD PHOTOS.

GOLIC: Greeny once recommended a book to me about baseball called *The Catcher in the Rye*. It didn't hold my attention—no pictures—and I put it down before it even got to the baseball part. The best part of sports books? Seeing the old players in their leatherheads, hockey goalies playing without protective masks, baseball legends with their lumpy mitts and wool uniforms, and a 12-year-old geek on a moped.

Greeny at his parents' summer house in 1979, revving his Honda Express II scooter.

Eight-year-old Mike Golic, with rosary, before his first holy communion in 1971.

Greeny's senior yearbook photo, 1985, Stuyvesant High School, New York City.

Michael Greenberg
Just do it. If you stop to think about it, you might change your mind . . . MG

Michael L. Golic

Golic's senior-year photo, 1981, St. Joseph High School, Cleveland.

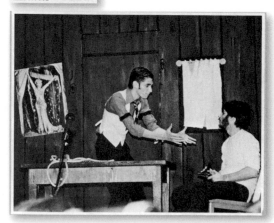

Greeny starring as Ali Hakim in a production of *Oklahoma!* His performance was panned by the student newspaper.

Golic (back row, second from right) with his high school wrestling team at the state championships, 1981.

Just The Facts

On Media Day, players and press searched for the true meaning of the Super Bowl

by RICK REILLY

MIKE GOLIC — EAGLES™

Greeny makes *Sports Illustrated*. That's him doing an exclusive interview with Bills defensive lineman Bruce Smith during Super Bowl week, 1993.

A 1992 Topps trading card of Eagles defensive lineman Mike Golic. Near-mint condition. Current selling price: 83 cents.

Greeny with his wife, Stacy, at one of the most hallowed grounds in sports, Wimbledon, 2005.

Golic with co-host Bruce Jacobs (left) at one of the most prestigious parking lots in Phoenix, for a KGME radio promotion, circa 1995.

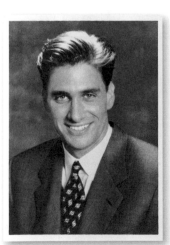

Greeny's first PR photo for ESPN, 1996. Suit by Prada. Tie by Hermés. Hair gel by Dep.

NFL 2Night host **Mark Malone** with analysts **Sean Salisbury** and **Mike Golic** (l to r).
Photo by: John Atashian

A clean and polished Mike Golic (right) on the set of <u>NFL 2Nite</u> during the program's rookie season, 1998.

ACKNOWLEDGMENTS

WE WOULD LIKE TO EXPRESS OUR SINCERE GRATITUDE to the many people who deserve it: George Bodenheimer, president of ESPN and the most powerful man in sports; Norby Williamson, who believed in our show from the start; Len Weiner, who put us together and saw the possibilities; Bruce Gilbert, who more than anyone figured out the best direction for our show; Traug Keller, who has been instrumental in our growth; and everyone at *Mike and Mike in the Morning*—especially Pete Gianesini, Justin Craig, Bob Picozzi, Scott "The Gnome" Shapiro, Liam Chapman, Curt "Joaquin" Kaplan, Rob "Stats" Guerrera, One-Name Jay Soderberg, Stosh Cienki, Mike Constantino, Gabby the Cleaning Lady, Chris Wondoloski, Steve Anthony, Seth Horwitz, Kim Murphy, Ed Headlam ("That's *Headlam*"), Paul Carr, Craig O'Brien, Paul Ryan, Lacy Sloan, Dan "Ubaldo" Filipone, Larry Young, and Joe Mead—for their tireless effort and for making us look good and sound smart. Any and all shortcomings are exclusively ours, not theirs.

Special thanks to Lou Oppenheim, who has been our friend, mentor, and trusted advisor for many, many years—KCM Forever!!!

Thanks to Libby McGuire, Kim Hovey, Mark Tavani, Paul Taunton, Christine Cabello, Cindy Murray and Joe Scalora at Random House and Gary Hoenig, Steve Wulf, Sandy DeShong, John Glenn, Chris Raymond, and Ellie Seifert at ESPN Books. Deep bows to our designer, Beth Tondreau, for making this book look better than we do.

We're also very grateful to Anni-Frid Lyngstad, Björn Ulvaeus, Benny Andersson, and Agnetha Fältskog. No explanation seems necessary.

And, at long last, thank you to our friends and families—aunts, uncles, cousins, nieces, nephews, in-laws, children, wives, and especially our parents, Harriet and Arnold Greenberg and Kate and Lou Golic—for their never-ending support.

ANDREW CHAIKIVSKY WOULD LIKE TO THANK: Chris Golic and Stacy Steponate Greenberg for their time, good spirits, and great stories; Arnold Greenberg, who followed through on every request and who has my lasting gratitude for urging me to get married. I'd also like to thank my agent on this project, Heather Schroder at ICM, for her wise counsel and assistance.

Several members of the extraordinary staff at *Mike and Mike*—especially The Gnome, Liam, Stats, and Joaquin—deserve a special round of applause for their great ideas and remarkable generosity. Joe Mead at ESPN.com helped immensely at several critical junctures, and Justin Craig, Pete Gianesini, Russell Baxter, and Bob Picozzi provided invaluable insights. Special thanks to Rich Arden, Brian Janes, Kevin Ingles, and Rob Phillips, and to Deatra Flanagan at the ESPN security desk.

Thank you, Mom and Dad, for your encouragement.

Finally, I'd like to thank my lovely wife, Liz, for her boundless patience and for her love.

PHOTOGRAPHY & ILLUSTRATION CREDITS

ABOUT THE AUTHORS

MIKE GREENBERG and **MIKE GOLIC** are co-hosts of *Mike and Mike in the Morning* on ESPN Radio and ESPN2.

A graduate of the Medill School of Journalism at Northwestern University, **MIKE GREENBERG** is also an anchor on ESPN's *SportsCenter* and was host of the ABC-TV game show *Duel*. His first book, the *New York Times* bestseller *Why My Wife Thinks I'm an Idiot*, was nominated for a Quill Award as one of the best sports books of 2006. He is married with two children.

Captain of the 1984 Notre Dame football team, **MIKE GOLIC** played defensive tackle for nine seasons in the NFL. While playing for the Philadelphia Eagles, he began his television career with a weekly feature, "Golic's Got It," on *The Randall Cunningham Show,* for which he was awarded a Mid-Atlantic Emmy. He joined ESPN in 1995 and continues to serve as an analyst for the network's NFL programming. Married with three children, Golic lives with his family in Connecticut.

ANDREW CHAIKIVSKY is a contributing editor to *Esquire* magazine. He lives in New York with his wife, Liz.

RULE **6.44**: MILK IT

STATE OF VERMONT
EXECUTIVE DEPARTMENT
A PROCLAMATION

WHEREAS, **Mike Greenberg** of ESPN's *Mike and Mike in the Morning* was raised among the cityscape and concrete of Manhattan and is what Vermonters would affectionately call "a flatlander"; and

WHEREAS, Vermonters are quite certain that prior to today, Mike would not have known the difference between a Holstein heifer and a Black Angus bull, or picked the cow out of a lineup of deer; and

WHEREAS, Mike lost his bet with Mike Golic on the NCAA tournament, and as a result was compelled this morning to milk a beautifully bedecked bovine beauty—whose name is Sox; and

WHEREAS, according to Sox, Greeny has a supple four-seam grip but could afford to spend a little more time down on the farm; and

WHEREAS, Vermonters are a kind and generous people who are delighted to highlight Mr. Greenberg's unique celebration of agriculture—one of our state's most important industries; and

WHEREAS, this udderly fun-filled agricultural tutorial may inspire Mike and Mike to visit us in Vermont to meet the Vermont Dairy Princess, enjoy the Strolling of the Heifers, or attend the Heifer Ball.

NOW, THEREFORE, I, James H. Douglas, Governor, do hereby proclaim Thursday, June 21, 2007, as MIKE GREENBERG DAY in Vermont and do hereby bestow upon him for this day the privilege of Honorary Resident of Vermont. Given under my hand and the Great Seal of the State of Vermont this 20th day of June, A.D. 2007.